CW01403542

READING WORDSWORTH

READING WORDSWORTH

J.H. Alexander

ROUTLEDGE & KEGAN PAUL
London

First published in 1987 by
Routledge & Kegan Paul Ltd
11 New Fetter Lane, London EC4P 4EE

Set in Bembo
by Columns Typesetting of Caversham
and printed in Great Britain
by T. J. Press (Padstow) Ltd.,
Padstow, Cornwall

British Library Cataloguing in Publication Data
Alexander, J.H. (John Huston)
'Reading Wordsworth'.
1. Wordsworth, William, 1770–1850
Criticism and interpretation
I. Title
821'.7   PR5881

ISBN 0–7102–1161–9

To Flora

. . . what we have loved
Others will love; and we may teach them how.

Contents

Preface

This short study of Wordsworth's poetry is addressed in the spirit of its epigraph to those who are encountering him for the first time, and to those who know his work but are at a loss to explain quite why it has impressed them, or (in the case of some readers) why it ought to have impressed them given the poet's acknowledged eminence. The works discussed have been selected to represent the main types of poetry written during the 'great decade' 1798–1807. Originality has not been my chief aim, and my debts to previous studies are incalculable. I have acknowledged specific borrowings when I have been aware of them, but there must be many cases where I have absorbed other readers' ideas so thoroughly that they seem a natural part of my own response: to all such original begetters, my heartfelt thanks.

Unless otherwise stated, all references to the poetry and the prose refer to Stephen Gill's 1984 Oxford Authors *William Wordsworth* (cited as Gill), and for versions and poems not included there I have generally used the Oxford Standard Authors *Poetical Works*, ed. Thomas Hutchinson, revised by Ernest de Selincourt (London, 1936: available as an Oxford Paperback).

I should like to thank Oxford University Press for permission to quote from *The Letters of William and Dorothy Wordsworth*, ed. Ernest de Selincourt (second edition, 1967–), and Fransisco Campbell Custódio and Ad. Donker (Pty) Ltd for permission to quote Roy Campbell's poem 'On Some South African Novelists'.

University of Aberdeen   J.H.A.

ix

CHAPTER 1

Introduction

Wordsworth's three supreme achievements are the *Lyrical Ballads* of 1798 and 1800 (together with 'The Ruined Cottage' and 'Peter Bell'), *The Prelude* as first completed in 1805, and the *Poems, in Two Volumes* published in 1807. Reading these works sympathetically and attentively is one of the most exciting of literary experiences, and one of the most demanding. Many people, however, find Wordsworth both unremarkable and dull, as they do his contemporary John Constable. For them Constable's *Cornfield* (or reproductions of it on chocolate boxes) and Wordsworth's 'Daffodils' (or memories of it from schooldays) are at best pleasant trifles, pallid banalities. Such objections to the poet are not of recent origin. The extensively revised *Prelude* was not published until 1850, shortly after Wordsworth's death, but the original reviewers of the *Lyrical Ballads* generally found them unremarkable, and within a few years, led by the Edinburgh critic Francis Jeffrey, they or their colleagues were mocking the 1807 *Poems* for their alleged puerility. From the outset, though, there were also a few readers who responded with a more appropriate fervour, among them William Hazlitt, Thomas De Quincey, and John Wilson ('Christopher North'):

> It had to me something of the effect that arises from the turning up of the fresh soil, or of the first welcome breath of Spring. (Hazlitt)

> . . . I may say in general, without the smallest exaggeration, that the whole aggregate of pleasure I have received from

1

some eight or nine other poets that I have been able to find
since the world began – falls infinitely short of what those
two enchanting volumes have singly afforded me. (De
Quincey)

Lyrical Ballads is . . . the book which I value next to my
Bible. (Wilson)[1]

The present study is offered in the conviction that one can
learn to read Wordsworth with a perception and enthusiasm
like theirs, and that his best work deserves all the effort
which can be brought to bear upon it.

The first requirement for reading Wordsworth well is
suggested by a characteristic which, allowing for the
difference between their respective arts, he shares with
Constable. Viewed from a distance, paintings such as *The
Cornfield* or *The Hay-Wain* may indeed be thought pleasant
but dull (one has seen that sort of thing a thousand times
before), but the spectator who approaches more closely and
begins to look rather than merely see will observe that every
inch of the canvas is thoroughly alive. It becomes clear that
the overall repose is made up of a host of intense local
excitements. So it is with Wordsworth, for example with
'Daffodils' (the popular title is half-sanctioned by the poet
himself).[2]

When a friend of Wordsworth's patron Sir George
Beaumont misread the earlier and simpler version of this
poem in the 1807 volumes (printed on page 104 below), the
poet was polite but firm in his correction:

Thanks for dear Lady B.'s transcript from your Friend's
Letter, – it is written with candour, but I must say a word or
two not in praise of it. 'Instances of what I mean,' says your
Friend, 'are to be found in a poem on a Daisy' (by the bye, it
is on *the* Daisy, a mighty difference). 'and on Daffodils
reflected in the Water' Is this accurately transcribed by Lady
Beaumont? If it be, what shall we think of criticism or
judgement founded upon and exemplified by a Poem which
must have been so inattentively perused? My Language is
precise, and, therefore, it would be false modesty to charge
myself with blame.

> – Beneath the trees,
> Ten thousand dancing in the *breeze*.
> The *waves beside* them danced, but they
> Outdid the *sparkling waves* in glee.

> Can expression be more distinct? And let me ask your Friend
> how it is possible for flowers to be *reflected* in water where
> there are *waves*. They may indeed in still water – but the very
> object of my poem is the trouble or agitation both of the
> flowers and the Water. I must needs respect the
> understanding of every one honoured by your friendship; but
> sincerity compels me to say that my Poems must be more
> nearly looked at before they can give rise to any remarks of
> much value, even from the strongest minds.[3]

Wordsworth's reaction makes it quite clear, as do many
other comments,[4] that he is very conscious of what he is
doing, that he is a very precise poet, and that an apparently
slight misreading can result in the reader missing the
imaginative and conceptual core of a poem. To peruse
Wordsworth quickly and carelessly is equivalent to viewing
Constable from a distance in casual perambulation, or in a
poor reproduction.

Byron called the long poem *The Excursion*, published in
1814, a 'drowsy, frowsy' piece,[5] and there are readers who
find even Wordsworth's greatest works of a decade earlier
decidedly soporific. (Charles Lamb, in general a sympathetic
and acute reader of Wordsworth as of most authors, once
pronounced the *Lyrical Ballads* 'but drowsy performances'.)[6]
Such misgivings, it may be felt, are reinforced by an entry
dated 29 April 1802 in the exquisite journal kept for short
periods by Wordsworth's sister Dorothy, who gave him, or
renewed in him, an acute sense of the details of the natural
world:

> We then went to John's Grove, sate a while at first.
> Afterwards William lay, and I lay in the trench under the
> fence – he with his eyes shut and listening to the waterfalls
> and the Birds. There was no one waterfall above another – it
> was a sound of waters in the air – the voice of the air. William
> heard me breathing and rustling now and then but we both
> lay still, and unseen by one another. He thought that it would

be as sweet thus to lie so in the grave, to hear the *peaceful* sounds of the earth and just to know that our dear friends were near.[7]

Much of Wordsworth's poetry seeks a repose, an extreme quietness, which approaches a timeless nirvana, and which may strike some readers as sepulchral. One can rarely quite say of him as one can of, and with, Blake that 'Energy is Eternal Delight'.[8] Something of the deep attraction which peace held for him is evident in his anguished exclamation to Robert Southey in 1805, shortly after the death of his beloved brother John Wordsworth:

> Oh! it makes the heart groan, that, with such a beautiful
> world as this to live in, and such a soul as that of man's is by
> nature and gift of God, we should go about on such errands
> as we do, destroying and laying waste; and ninety-nine of us
> in a hundred never easy in any road that travels towards peace
> and quietness![9]

The causes of the decline in Wordsworth's highest creative powers after 1807 are complex and still only very imperfectly understood, but one of them was certainly this seeking a 'repose which ever is the same' as the 'Ode to Duty' of 1807 has it. James Averill, linking Wordsworth with the sentimental tradition, says that in his poetry 'guilt, fear, grief, remembered terror, or intense response to nature, – virtually any powerful emotion it would seem – is able to move the mind to profound tranquillity. . . . The subsequent calm is the result of a mind made self-conscious by the presence of emotion.'[10] But for the sympathetic reader, to succumb too quickly to the quietness, the trancelike state, which Wordsworth can induce is to be in danger of missing the very considerable energy of his creative powers at their peak. It may indeed be that the poet of the great decade exhausted himself for ever in the fierce intellectual and emotional throes of composition – and, particularly stressful for him, of revision. In many of his best works energy and repose coexist, and are experienced simultaneously rather than successively. 'They have a stillness which does not deny movement, and movement which contains stillness.'[11]

4

From Nature doth emotion come, and moods
Of calmness equally are Nature's gift,
This is her glory; these two attributes
Are sister horns that constitute her strength;
This twofold influence is the sun and shower
Of all her bounties, both in origin
And end alike benignant. Hence it is,
That Genius, which exists by interchange
Of peace and excitation, finds in her
His best and purest Friend, from her receives
That energy by which he seeks the truth,
Is rouzed, aspires, grasps, struggles, wishes, craves,
From her that happy stillness of the mind
Which fits him to receive it, when unsought.

(Prelude, XII, 1–14)

There are obvious and attractive vigours in such poems as 'Goody Blake and Harry Gill' from the 1798 *Lyrical Ballads* or 'Written in March' from the 1807 *Poems*, but Wordsworth's energy is often more subtly put forth. Frequently, one of the best ways of discerning such manifestations is to compare the original version of his poems with later revisions, for although he remained a fine craftsman and sometimes improved his early poems in later life, he also lost contact to a distressing extent with the imaginative vigour of his prime. The notorious review of the 1807 *Poems* in the *Edinburgh Review* by Francis Jeffrey,[12] who recognised Wordsworth's genius but thought that it was seriously misdirected towards low or unimportant subjects presented in childish language, had a disastrous effect on Wordsworth's reputation (and his purse) for the next fifteen years or so. Extraordinary to relate, in the course of time Wordsworth altered almost every line to which Jeffrey had taken exception in accordance with the critic's strictures, so that the original distinguishing energy seeped out and was lost. One of the most striking casualties of this sorry process was the poem 'Beggars', in which Wordsworth describes his encounter with a striking gypsy woman. Jeffrey pronounced this poem 'a very paragon of silliness and affectation' and quoted the third stanza, in which Wordsworth originally wrote in 1802, and printed in 1807, this description of her:

5

> Before me begging did she stand,
> Pouring out sorrows like a sea;
> Grief after grief; – on English Land
> Such woes I knew could never be.

In the 1827 revision this became:

> Her suit no faltering scruples checked;
> Forth did she pour, in current free,
> Tales that could challenge no respect
> But from a blind credulity.

In revision Wordsworth has lost the impressive image of the sorrows pouring out 'like a sea': not *the* sea, but *a* particular, visualised sea – wave after wave, grief upon grief. In 1828 Barron Field rightly criticised these and other alterations, indicating that Wordsworth had 'a little disposition in your alterations to mitigate that simplicity of speech, which you taught us was the true language of the heart, and to make some tardy sacrifice at the shrine of poetic diction; and thus, after having "created the taste by which you have been enjoyed", in a small degree deserting your disciples'. Wordsworth replied that 'sea' clashed with the last line of the stanza, 'was beautiful to see'.[13] This is a fair point, made by a still distinguished craftsman, but the remedy is drastic indeed, and by 1845 he had eliminated the last trace of the original vigour:

> Advancing, forth she stretched her hand
> And begged an alms with doleful plea
> That ceased not.

Wordsworth told Barron Field that his aim in altering the poem had been to give it 'more elegance and dignity'. One is reminded of Roy Campbell's celebrated aphorism 'On Some South African Novelists':

> You praise the firm restraint with which they write –
> I'm with you there, of course:
> They use the snaffle and the curb all right,
> But where's the bloody horse?

Wordsworth's characteristic energy is often discernible in his handling of the smallest and commonest words. The power of 'a sea' in 'Beggars' is paralleled by numerous instances. In this sample the relevant words are italicised:

> One summer-day I chanced to see
> This old man doing all he could
> *About* the root of an old tree.

> Whole summer fields are thine by right;
> And Autumn, melancholy Wight!
> Doth in thy crimson head delight
>   When rains *are* on thee.

> . . . of all that we behold
> *From* this green earth.

> And thine is, *too*, the last green field
>   That Lucy's eyes surveyed![14]

That Wordsworth was fully aware of the energetic charge which the meanest words can be made to carry is most strikingly demonstrated by a climactic bravura line from his account of the crossing of the Alps in Book VI of *The Prelude* (566–72):

> The unfettered clouds and region of the heavens,
> Tumult and peace, the darkness and the light
> Were all like workings of one mind, the features
> Of the same face, blossoms upon one tree,
> Characters of the great Apocalypse,
> The types and symbols of Eternity,
> Of first and last, and midst, and without end.

That last line alludes clearly to the hymn sung by Adam and Eve in *Paradise Lost* (V, 164–5):

> . . . join all ye creatures to extol
> Him first, him last, him midst, and without end.

To replace God by an ampersand might strike some as blasphemous. It certainly indicates that the many connecting 'And's in Wordsworth are not mere empty spaces but conductors through which can be discerned, in the act of leaping, the spark of an energy which might, in some sense, be termed divine.

The reader should be aware that apparently identical

usages of simple words can carry different forces. Wordsworth was accustomed to seeing the same Cumbrian
mountains change radically in varied seasons, lights, and
atmospheric conditions, and his words shift beneath one's
gaze in an analogous fashion.[15] In the second stanza of 'It
is the first mild day of March',

> There is a blessing in the air,
> Which seems a sense of joy to yield
> To the bare trees, and mountains bare,
> And grass in the green field,

'bare trees' and 'mountains bare' vary the connotations of
the adjective (mountains are not bare in quite the same way
as trees are) and make it possible for the corresponding
adjective 'green' to strike with fresh force in the final line. A
slightly different point has been made by Roger Murray.
Near the beginning of 'Resolution and Independence'
Wordsworth describes a hare in vivid motion:

> The Hare is running races in her mirth;
> And with her feet she from the plashy earth
> Raises a mist; which, glittering in the sun,
> Runs with her all the way, wherever she doth run.
>
> (11–14)

Murray notes: 'The first "runs" borrows some of its force
from the second, that of the hare, and thus heightens our
sense that the mist is something alive and volitional,' that
there is a pervasive natural blessing.[16]

Words which are at first sight parallel will be found on
careful reading to demand a change of response, as in the
celebrated lines from 'Tintern Abbey':

> . . . something far more deeply interfused,
> Whose dwelling is the light of setting suns,
> And the round ocean, and the living air,
> And the blue sky, and in the mind of man.
>
> (97–100)

Here the plural 'suns', the 'round' ocean, and the 'living' air
all maintain the reader's alertness, so that one sees what
might otherwise be a cliché in 'blue sky' as if with a newly
created faculty, the more vividly against the prevailing green

of the poem. F.J. Hugo comments: 'The whole effect is to bring home to us an image of diverse elements which together create the containing and sustaining medium of life.'[17] The process is concluded by distinguishing the 'mind of man' from the other habitations of the 'something' (the 'presence') by means of the preposition 'in', so as to suggest a uniquely human complexity.[18]

Some who have read Wordsworth carefully and discovered or sensed his energy may nevertheless be worried by his deliberate self-limitation. After some experience in France of the great public events associated with the Revolution during the 1790s, and a period of intense intellectual and emotional disorientation, he retired to the country, living in Dorset and Somerset for a few years and then (after an unsociable few months in Germany) settling permanently at Christmas 1799 in the English Lake District where he had grown up (Gill, pp. xxvii–xxviii). It is possible to regard this retirement as a retreat from responsibilities, an averting of the 'ken / From half of human fate', as Matthew Arnold was to put it, and to wish with Byron that Wordsworth would change his lakes for ocean.[19] But to regard this self-limitation negatively would be to underestimate two important factors.

In the first place, Wordsworth is always a moral writer, which involves 'carrying every where with him relationship and love' (Gill, p. 606), and his retirement, though by no means unproblematic or unambiguous, is a positive moral and artistic statement. It involves a criticism of metropolitan life with its artificial homogenised culture, its snobberies, its inhumanity, its modishness, and above all its appetite for extravagant and sensational entertainment. In the Preface which Wordsworth wrote for the second edition of *Lyrical Ballads* in 1800 (at Coleridge's prompting, and with an unquantifiable but pronounced Coleridgean input) he made a point of warning his readers about the dangers of 'the encreasing accumulation of men in cities, where the uniformity of their occupations produces a craving for extraordinary incident, which the rapid communication of intelligence hourly gratifies'. The consequence for literature is that 'the invaluable works of our elder writers, I had almost said the works of Shakespeare and Milton, are driven

into neglect by frantic novels, sickly and stupid German
Tragedies, and deluges of idle and extravagant stories in
verse' (Gill, p. 599). In his art as in his life Wordsworth
rejects the sensational, the easy, the superficial. He will not
tell exciting stories, stimulate facile emotions, or write about
stirring adventures. Even when considering the best productions of that sort, as in Scott and Byron, Wordsworth makes
it clear that his preferences lie elsewhere. Acknowledging
receipt of Scott's medieval narrative poem *Marmion* he
writes, a little too carefully: 'Thank you for Marmion which
I have read with lively pleasure – I think your end has been
attained; that it is not in every respect the end which I
should wish you to propose to yourself, you will be well
aware from what you know of my notions of composition,
both as to matter and manner.'[20] In the lyrical ballad 'Simon
Lee, the Old Huntsman', he teases those readers who are
expecting a sensational story. After eight stanzas describing
Simon and his wife Ruth, Wordsworth knows, some of his
polite audience will be growing impatient, and he addresses
these 'gentle' readers directly:

> My gentle reader, I perceive
> How patiently you've waited,
> And I'm afraid that you expect
> Some tale will be related.
>
> O reader! had you in your mind
> Such stores as silent thought can bring,
> O gentle reader! you would find
> A tale in every thing.
> What more I have to say is short,
> I hope you'll kindly take it;
> It is no tale; but should you think,
> Perhaps a tale you'll make it.
>
> (69–80)

That is plain speaking, an extreme example from among
many passages where one should be asking what Wordsworth is deliberately doing to his readers.[21] He is accusing
some at least of them of being unthinking, of lacking those
stores of meditative experience which would enable them to
discern in the apparently dull subject an excitement to rival,

and indeed surpass, anything in a more conventionally stimulating narrative. The 'moving accident' is not his trade, as he puts it in 'Hart-Leap Well':

> To curl the blood I have no ready arts;
> 'Tis my delight, alone in summer shade,
> To pipe a simple song to thinking hearts.

> (97–100)

Writing to Coleridge in 1798 about Gottfried August Bürger's ballads, Wordsworth remarked that 'incidents are among the lowest allurements of poetry', and ten years later he observed to the same friend apropos of *The White Doe of Rylstone*:

> If he [a man of genius] is to be a Dramatist, let him crowd his scene with gross and visible action; but if a narrative Poet, if the poet is to be predominant over the Dramatist, – then let him see if there are no victories in the world of spirit, no changes, no commotions, no revolutions there, no fluxes and refluxes of the thoughts which may be made interesting by modest combination with the stiller actions of the bodily frame, or with the gentler movements and milder appearances of society and social intercourse, or the still more mild and gentle solicitations of irrational and inanimate nature.[22]

Significance, relationship, the spiritual interpretation of life are at the heart of Wordsworth's conception of the moral:

> To every natural form, rock, fruit or flower,
> Even the loose stones that cover the high-way,
> I gave a moral life, I saw them feel,
> Or linked them to some feeling: the great mass
> Lay bedded in a quickening soul and all
> That I beheld respired with inward meaning.[23]

The 'thinking heart' will be able to feel and interpret Wordsworth's minimalism, finding a profound satisfaction in apparently impoverished subject matter and apparently elementary style.

The chief corollary of this moral and artistic statement of principle is Wordsworth's implicit assertion that his subject matter is entirely commensurate with his art, that it is worthy of the full expenditure of a major artist's

11

endowment: indeed, that, if anything, his art is actually inadequate to the full exploration of his experience of the country folk and their natural surroundings. The revolutionary nature of the claim may be difficult to appreciate now, but this is because Wordsworth and his contemporaries, and their Victorian successors, have carried the revolution through and modern readers are all children of that revolution, accepting without thinking that the everyday is endlessly fascinating. In his account of the impact which Wordsworth's earliest works made on him, Coleridge summed up much of what Wordsworth was about. He was impressed by the 'freedom from false taste' which he detected in the earliest works and saw developed in the major achievements, but what really

> made so unusual an impression on my feelings immediately,
> and subsequently on my judgement . . . was the union of
> deep feeling with profound thought; the fine balance of truth
> in observing with the imaginative faculty in modifying the
> objects observed; and above all the original gift of spreading
> the tone, the *atmosphere*, and with it the depth and height of
> the ideal world [i.e. the world of ideas] around forms,
> incidents, and situations, of which, for the common view,
> custom had bedimmed all the lustre, had dried up the sparkle
> and the dew drops.[24]

Wordsworth's aim, as Coleridge saw, is nothing less than to strip the whole of everyday experience of its over-familiar patina, to 'defamiliarise' it, to alert his readers to the wonder and inexhaustible richness of ordinary people, of the natural world, of their own imaginative minds, and of the living and moral relationships among these three elements. He believes that by concentrating on these features his poetry will avoid the merely local and the temporary and will become an enduring force like one of Nature's. Although most of his modern readers will be urban, and some of them may find his determined rurality unsettling, there is reason to believe that his hope has been justified, at any rate in part: 'Daffodils' is one of the very few poems that a large number of people of very widely differing backgrounds and educational attainments know and love. Wordsworth would have attached great importance to such diffusion, since he hoped that some of his poems might attain wide popularity among the less literate members of society.[25] In the prologue to the strange but impressive lyrical ballad 'Peter Bell' as published in 1819 (it was written in 1798, but extensively revised in manuscript over a period of years) Wordsworth rejects the temptation to write about remote exotic landscapes and 'the realm of Faery' and proclaims:

> 'Long have I loved what I behold,
> The night that calms, the day that cheers;
> The common growth of mother-earth
> Suffices me – her tears, her mirth,
> Her humblest mirth and tears.
>
> 'The dragon's wing, the magic ring,
> I shall not covet for my dower,
> If I along that lowly way
> With sympathetic heart may stray,
> And with a soul of power.
>
> 'These given, what more need I desire
> To stir, to soothe, or elevate?
> What nobler marvels than the mind
> May in life's daily prospect find,
> May find or there create?'
>
> (131–45)

'Common' is a favourite campaigning word in Wordsworth's poetry, constantly reminding the reader of his belief in the moral and aesthetic value of the ordinary.[26]

The main emphasis in this study will be on Wordsworth's characteristic way with words, but it will be clear throughout that the process of learning to appreciate his distinctive style is not only an aesthetic but a moral education. The reader is asked to slow down, to take time to observe, to feel, and to think. Matthew Arnold was of course right: there are vast areas of experience which Wordsworth deliberately neglects and which other writers have dealt with. But he is a poet of great energy as well as great calm, deep fears as well as profound joy, good humour as well as high seriousness, a lively interest in his neighbours as well as the most thorough self-absorption; a writer who could in the same period compose the great shifting cellular organism which is *The Prelude*, and that most finely honed and succinct of elegiac lyrics, the eight-line 'A slumber did my spirit seal'.

To the list of injunctions in the preceding paragraph there are two more to be added. Firstly: read aloud. A book cannot do this; it can only urge that it be done. Wordsworth often composed his poems while walking in the open air, 'wi' a girt voice bumming awaay fit to flayte aw tho childer to death ameaast',[27] and he habitually read them to his family circle. All of his works from shortest lyric, through lyrical ballad, to *The Prelude* come fully to life only when they are heard, aloud or at least in the mind's ear. As a brief experiment, the reader may care to recite the following short poem without haste, observing the scrupulous carefulness of the diction and the delicate rhythm, and pondering the ambiguous effect (deflationary? pacifist? shocking? pathetic?) of the last six lines with their 'found poem' which follows very closely, one imagines, the actual words which Wordsworth heard:

Old Man Travelling;
Animal Tranquillity and Decay,
A Sketch

The little hedge-row birds,
That peck along the road, regard him not.
He travels on, and in his face, his step,
His gait, is one expression; every limb,
His look and bending figure, all bespeak
A man who does not move with pain, but moves
With thought – He is insensibly subdued
To settled quiet; he is one by whom
All effort seems forgotten, one to whom
Long patience has such mild composure given,
That patience now doth seem a thing, of which
He hath no need. He is by nature led
To peace so perfect, that the young behold
With envy, what the old man hardly feels.
– I asked him whither he was bound, and what
The object of his journey; he replied
'Sir! I am going many miles to take

'A last leave of my son, a mariner,
'Who from a sea-fight has been brought to Falmouth,
And there is dying in an hospital.'

(Any reader who, after due consideration, finds these concluding lines merely incongruous has Wordsworth's authority for omitting them, as in printings after 1805.)

The final injunction must be a suggestion that if possible the reader should visit the Lake District. In an age which directs its attention so puritanically to the words on the page this may seem a quaint idea, but it remains true that 'One impulse from a vernal wood'[28] *may* be more illuminating than any number of critical works. The impulse may be sublime: a wholly unsought sudden awareness of mountainous 'presence' at Castlerigg Stone Circle after a hard day's cycling, for instance. Whether the visitor chooses to interpret such experiences as psychological phenomena or more mystically, they are the true Wordsworthian spots of time, and may strike at any moment. Or it may be more gentle and subtle: a becoming aware by Grasmere lake that the early morning sun is 'steeping' the fern as it does in the Westminster Bridge sonnet. The reader may return to the poetry with an eye more alert to those delicate details for which Wordsworth does not often receive credit:

– 'Twas that delightful season, when the broom,
Full flowered, and visible on every steep,
Along the copses runs in veins of gold.

There, sometimes doth a leaping Fish
Send through the Tarn a lonely chear.

But see! where'er the hailstones drop
The withered leaves all skip and hop.[29]

To explore the Wordsworthian haunts with David McCracken's guide *Wordsworth and the Lake District*,[30] to examine the influential gardens at Dove Cottage and Rydal Mount,[31] to meditate in Rydal church upon Wordsworth's later career, to stand beside the family's graves in Grasmere churchyard, to hear the voices of innumerable becks and forces after heavy rain, to 'read' the Lake District – its landscape, trees, and buildings – in the light of Wordsworth's own *Guide through the Lakes* and link his detailed concerns with modern environmental issues:[32] to do all of these is immeasurably to enrich one's understanding of those words on the page to which the study now returns.

CHAPTER 2

Lyrical Ballads
(1798 and 1800)

I

The Advertisement prefixed to *Lyrical Ballads, with a few other poems* in 1798 implies that this is intended to be avant-garde literature, poetry pushing out to new frontiers:

> The majority of the following poems are to be considered as experiments. They were written chiefly with a view to ascertain how far the language of conversation in the middle and lower classes of society is adapted to the purposes of poetic pleasure. Readers accustomed to the gaudiness and inane phraseology of many modern writers, if they persist in reading this book to its conclusion, will perhaps frequently have to struggle with feelings of strangeness and aukwardness: they will look round for poetry, and will be induced to enquire by what species of courtesy these attempts can be permitted to assume that title. It is desirable that such readers, for their own sakes, should not suffer the solitary word Poetry, a word of very disputed meaning, to stand in the way of their gratification; but that, while they are perusing this book, they should ask themselves if it contains a natural delineation of human passions, human characters, and human incidents; and if the answer be favorable to the author's wishes, that they should consent to be pleased in spite of that most dreadful enemy to our pleasures, our own pre-established codes of decision. (Gill, p. 591)

But the paragraph which follows this bold assertion qualifies it by suggesting that the experiment aims to recapture

17

something of the freedom of 'our elder writers' (that is, most notably, Chaucer and the great ballad writers) to use the simplest language for poetic purposes. Wordsworth and Coleridge are thus not, in their experimentation, breaking their implied contract with the reader, and those who are prepared to put aside their expectations of superficially dignified language and their class bias will find themselves responding to passions, characters, and incidents involving men and women not wholly unlike themselves.

The immediate reception accorded the volume was very mixed. (It must be borne in mind that the ballads proper account for only half the publication: there are also personal and dramatic lyrics, dialogues, and blank verse meditations culminating in 'Tintern Abbey'.) Robert Southey, who should have known better, objected to the eminence given to uninteresting subjects.[1] Dr Charles Burney, the musicologist and doyen of letters, provided a characteristically receptive but somewhat cautious analysis, taking up Wordsworth's challenge in the Advertisement:

> Though we have been extremely entertained with the fancy, the facility, and (in general) the sentiments, of these pieces, we cannot regard them as *poetry*, of a class to be cultivated at the expence of a higher species of versification, unknown in our language at the time when our elder writers, whom this author condescends to imitate, wrote their ballads.[2]

The reviewer in *The British Critic*, possibly Francis Wrangham, was the most perceptive of the formal critics. He understood fully what the author (he appears to think that the whole volume may be by Coleridge) was basically about – that is, recalling 'our poetry from the fantastical excess of refinement, to simplicity and nature' – and judged that he had triumphantly attained his objective:

> . . . we think that in general the author has succeeded in attaining that judicious degree of simplicity, which accommodates itself with ease even to the sublime. It is not by pomp of words, but by energy of thought, that sublimity is most successfully achieved; and we infinitely prefer the simplicity even of the most unadorned tale in this volume, to all the meretricious frippery of the *Darwinian* taste.[3]

This perceptive acceptance was echoed by the young enthusiasts quoted in the preceding chapter. John Wilson, barely seventeen, wrote to Wordsworth in May 1802: 'You do not write merely for the pleasure of philosophers and men of improved taste, but for all who think, for all who feel', and William Hazlitt sensed in 1798 'a new style and a new spirit in poetry'.[4]

Some of Wordsworth's original readers did not see that anything very remarkable had happened in the *Lyrical Ballads*; for others, there had been a revolution. It helps towards an understanding of the ballads especially (and casts some light also on the 'few other poems') to ask why there should have been such varied reactions.

For several years before 1798, a host of poetasters had been contributing to the magazines literary ballads in simple styles concerning pathetic, impoverished characters.[5] When Wordsworth's lyrical ballads are compared with the contents of these magazines two major differences appear, and it is these which may properly be deemed revolutionary. In the first place, encouraged no doubt by the example of Robert Burns two decades earlier, Wordsworth maintains that his ballads are not merely minor entertainments but major literature, challenging comparison with 'our elder poets'. This claim, massively reinforced by the 1800–2 Preface, was a startling one when taken seriously, as Francis Jeffrey in attack and Wrangham, Wilson, Hazlitt, and De Quincey in appreciation all recognised. It would seem that Wordsworth has won this particular argument and has created the taste by which he, and thousands of more recent poets dealing with the ordinary in ordinary language, are to be appreciated. But if such minimalist art is to excite and please it must be highly crafted and involve its own sorts of complexity, and it is here that the other crucial difference (or set of differences) between Wordsworth and his minor contemporaries becomes important. One will search the magazines in vain for the close observation, the linguistic and structural distinction, the humour, and supremely perhaps the sense of strangeness, which are woven together in Wordsworth's ballads. They are a most notable example of that combination of apparent extreme simplicity with profound artfulness which distinguishes much literature of the Romantic period in Germany and Britain. Hazlitt talked of 'the unaccountable mixture of seeming simplicity and real abstruseness' in the *Lyrical Ballads* and added: 'Fools have laughed at, wise men scarcely understand them.'[6]

Four lyrical ballads: 'Simon Lee, the Old Huntsman', 'Goody Blake and Harry Gill', 'The Thorn', and 'The Idiot Boy'

Although the exact boundary between the 'lyrical ballads' and the 'few other poems' in the 1798 volume can be debated, there can be no doubt that the two short poems 'Simon Lee, the Old Huntsman' and 'Goody Blake and Harry Gill' and the two longer pieces 'The Thorn' and 'The Idiot Boy' belong to the former category. Wordsworth makes the principal significance of the novel compound term 'lyrical ballads' quite clear in the 1800 Preface:

> . . . I should mention one other circumstance which
> distinguishes these Poems from the popular Poetry of the
> day; it is this, that the feeling therein developed gives
> importance to the action and situation, and not the action and
> situation to the feeling. (Gill, p. 599)

The first chapter noted how in 'Simon Lee, the Old Huntsman' Wordsworth deliberately draws the polite reader's attention to the absence of an exciting or sensational story. The situation which he presents is potentially sentimental, but unlike many of his minor contemporaries he carefully keeps the sentimental at bay. Physically, Simon is unidealised:

> Full five and twenty years he lived
> A running huntsman merry;
> And, though he has but one eye left,
> His cheek is like a cherry.

(13–16)

That penultimate line works against the 'merry England' clichés as Wordsworth jumbles together the contrasts between vital past and diminished present. (In later revision he was to dispose of the younger Simon before depicting his present state, as well as eliminating the crucial detail about the missing eye, so that the poem becomes more logical but less robust.)[7] Even the picture of the past is touched with a vigour far beyond the hackneyed: 'often, ere the race was done, / He reeled and was stone-blind' (43–4). The sentimental is further guarded against by the humour of Simon's uncertainty or duplicity about his age in the first stanza and by the grotesque geriatric comedy:

> And he is lean and he is sick,
> His little body's half awry;
> His ancles they are swoln and thick;
> His legs are thin and dry.
>
> (33–6)

The address to the reader continues this anti-sentimental process, which is completed in the clear-sighted conclusion, avoiding any hint of a cliché moral and requiring active interpretation by the instructed and perceptive reader:

> – I've heard of hearts unkind, kind deeds
> With coldness still returning.
> Alas! the gratitude of men
> Has oftner left me mourning.

The reader has been kept alert throughout the poem, tempted with clichés but denied their easy comforts, and the result is a strong and original piece which made two very specific moral and social points for its original readers, opposing both William Godwin's dismissal of gratitude as 'no part of justice or virtue' and the enclosure of that common land which is so vital to Simon Lee.[8]

The curious story which Wordsworth found in the notes to Erasmus Darwin's poem *Zoönomia* and transformed into 'Goody Blake and Harry Gill' has a more obvious and simple moral, leaving the reader free to enjoy the grotesqueness of the narration with its delighted play on warmth and cold. The crucial word, the seed from which the poem grows, is 'chatter'. From it derives the pattern of lively feminine rhymes which begin each stanza: 'matter'/'chatter' is clearly echoed first in 'fetter'/'met her' and then after their return in the penultimate stanza in the final 'utters'/'mutters'. At the heart of the poem is a tension between these feminine initial rhymes and the often grimly insistent masculine rhymes on 'poor' (21), 'alone' (36), 'dead' (that is, 'without fire', 45), 'sick' (53), 'ache' (58), 'chill' (106), and 'old'/'cold' (122/4). Harry's erstwhile energy is summed up in the word 'lusty' which is cunningly transferred to poor Goody's world when the winds provide her with firewood and brief joy:

> Oh joy for her! when e'er in winter
> The winds at night had made a rout,
> And scattered many a lusty splinter,
> And many a rotten bough about.
>
> (49-52)

The old man's energy is carried over into the excess of his attempts to regain warmth (5-8), and the grotesque vigour of his ailment: 'still his jaws and teeth they clatter, / Like a loose casement in the wind' (115-16). A more zestful poem has yet to be penned.

'The Thorn' is a more ambitious poem than the two ballads so far considered, and in the 1800 edition Wordsworth provided it with an elaborate exegetical note of the greatest interest. But it is best to start with the remark which he made to Isabella Fenwick when she was compiling her invaluable notes in his later years:

> Arose out of my observing, on the ridge of Quantock Hill,
> on a stormy day, a thorn which I had often passed in calm
> and bright weather without noticing it. I said to myself,
> 'Cannot I by some invention do as much to make this Thorn
> permanently an impressive object as the storm has made it to
> my eyes at this moment?' I began the poem accordingly and
> composed it with great rapidity. (Gill, p. 688)

So this poem, with its strongly characterised narrator and his weird story, is a way of transferring to the reader something of Wordsworth's response to the isolated thorn as perceived under a particular set of atmospheric conditions.[9] What the poet and the captain have seen is a numinous spot, an object (or two objects: Dorothy Wordsworth in her Alfoxden Journal for 20 April 1798 refers to 'the thorn, and the "little muddy pond"') which encapsulates a weird elemental natural combat, between erect thorn and mosses struggling to drag it down to the earth. This tension is reinforced in the opening stanza by the comparisons with a two years' child and a stone: the thorn exists between the human and the inanimate worlds.

Wordsworth's way of conjuring up this scene is highly sophisticated, though the medium may be a 'barbaric yawp', a quasi-primitive expression of neurosis and anguish.[10] The poem's most striking technical feature is its strongly developed narrator. Already in the 1798 Advertisement Wordsworth had felt it necessary to draw the reader's attention to this feature, and in the 1800 note (Gill, pp. 593-4) he goes so far as to suggest that he should really have provided an introductory poem. Never having been in the mood to write this introductory poem well, he furnishes instead a thumbnail sketch of the type of person represented by the narrator:

> The character which I have here introduced speaking is sufficiently common. The Reader will perhaps have a general notion of it, if he has ever known a man, a Captain of a small trading vessel for example, who being past the middle age of life, had retired upon an annuity or small independent income to some village or country town of which he was not a native, or in which he had not been accustomed to live. Such men having little to do become credulous and talkative from indolence; and from the same cause, and other predisposing causes by which is is probable that such men may have been affected, they are prone to superstition. On which account it appeared to me proper to select a character like this to exhibit some of the general laws by which superstition acts upon the mind. Superstitious men are almost always men of slow faculties and deep feelings; their minds are not loose but adhesive; they have a reasonable share of imagination, by which word I mean the faculty which produces impressive effects out of simple elements; but they are utterly destitute of fancy, the power by which pleasure and surprize are excited by sudden varieties of situation and an accumulated imagery.

Francis Jeffrey was particularly amused by the opening of that passage, and one may conjecture that the poet is writing with something of a twinkle in his eye; but the device is an intriguing one, and Wordsworth's explanation helps us to understand a good deal of its potential effectiveness. The sea-captain is gullible, slow, loquacious, and of an 'adhesive' mind: that is to say, obsessive. Like Coleridge's Ancient Mariner he buttonholes his listener with an abrupt opening, going straight to the heart of his obsession: 'There is a thorn'. But unlike the Mariner he is an incompetent narrator. He keeps on repeating himself, and he cannot avoid anticipating his main point:

> This heap of earth o'ergrown with moss
> Which close beside the thorn you see,
> So fresh in all its beauteous dyes,
> Is like an infant's grave in size
> As like as like can be:
> But never, never any where,
> An infant's grave was half so fair.

(49–55)

Coleridge complained in his *Biographia Literaria* about this eddying motion in Wordsworth's poetry, but it has been recognised that the obsessive circling round a spot and an object is one way of suggesting the ultimate mystery and inexplicability of their power to attract and to possess the imagination.[11] It is partly by means of this obsessive circling, this disruption of straightforward linear narrative, that the simple thorn is made as impressive in the reader's eye as it had been for Wordsworth and his narrator.

The circularity of movement is reinforced by the verbal repetitiveness, the apparent tautology, and here again Wordsworth's 1800 note is illuminating as he challenges an educated readership:

There is a numerous class of readers who imagine that the same words cannot be repeated without tautology: this is a great error: virtual tautology is much oftener produced by using different words when the meaning is exactly the same. Words, a Poet's words more particularly, ought to be weighed in the balance of feeling and not measured by the space which they occupy upon paper. For the Reader cannot be too often reminded that Poetry is passion: it is the history or science of feelings: now every man must know that an attempt is rarely made to communicate impassioned feelings without something of an accompanying consciousness of the inadequateness of our own powers, or the deficiencies of language. During such efforts there will be a craving in the mind, and as long as it is unsatisfied the Speaker will cling to the same words, or words of the same character. There are also various other reasons why repetition and apparent tautology are frequently beauties of the highest kind. Among the chief of these reasons is the interest which the mind attaches to words, not only as symbols of the passion, but as *things*, active and efficient, which are of themselves part of the passion. And further, from a spirit of fondness, exultation, and gratitude, the mind luxuriates in the repetition of words which appear successfully to communicate its feelings. The truth of these remarks might be shewn by innumerable passages from the Bible and from the impassioned poetry of every nation.

Wordsworth believed that his poetry should draw on the banal but deeply felt clichés which ordinary people use at moments of greatest passion. By repeating in particular Martha Ray's word 'misery' he wishes it to become as it were a substantial thing, an object with which the tongue and brain become familiar by repeated recitation so that it burns itself into the memory. The closest modern parallel, as often with Wordsworth, is with Samuel Beckett, whose elemental stage images and repeated phrases are not easily forgotten. The significance of Wordsworth's note to 'The Thorn' extends far beyond that poem; for along with Bunyan, Richardson, and Beckett he is among the great obsessive writers in English.

The 1800 note has one other point to make, a difficult observation concerning the choice of a 'Lyrical and rapid Metre' apparently inappropriate for this subject:

> It was necessary that the Poem, to be natural, should in reality move slowly; yet I hoped, that, by the aid of the metre, to those who should at all enter into the spirit of the Poem, it would appear to move quickly.

This may or may not be rationalising after the event, but the conflicting impressions of rapidity and extreme slowness are undoubtedly important for the work's impact. It was

25

composed, Wordsworth says, 'with great rapidity', and the metre reflects this sense of artistic urgency and indeed of the narrator's pressing need to communicate his experience. Against this, the repetitions and circlings convey a static effect, a haunted stillness.

The narration is, as always in Wordsworth, richly varied within its apparent monotony. It is amusing as well as portentous and haunting. The captain's computations are no doubt partly a stratagem to avoid being overwhelmed by the horror: like Marlow travelling up the Congo in Conrad's *Heart of Darkness* Wordsworth's sea-captain makes sure that he has work to do, measuring 'five yards', 'three yards', 'three feet long, and two feet wide', 'half a foot in height' (27–37). There is no reason to suppress a smile at this point. It was only after 1815 that Wordsworth bowed to solemn pressure and changed lines 32 and 33 to read:

> Though but of compass small, and bare
> To thirsty suns and parching air.

That is too literary for the captain. His lyricism is more basic and more impressive:

> And she is known to every star,
> And every wind that blows.

> (69–70)

> And there she sits, until the moon
> Through half the clear blue sky will go.

> (203–4)

The primitive grotesque force of the narrator's language also came in for censorship. Martha's reaction to her jilting had originally been described thus:

> A cruel, cruel fire, they say,
> Into her bones was sent:
> It dried her body like a cinder,
> And almost turned her brain to tinder.

> (129–32)

How much more vital and effective that is than the faded language of its 1815 replacement:

A pang of pitiless dismay
Into her soul was sent;
A fire was kindled in her breast,
Which might not burn itself to rest.

Obsessive, pedantic, haunting, humorous, lyrical, impassioned, a poem about a thorn, about a particular psychological cast of mind, about the origin of superstitions, about creation from almost nothing, 'The Thorn' had also a strong personal significance for the poet. It has been observed how odd it is, to say the least, that Wordsworth should give the jilted mother the name of Martha Ray, the mother of his friend Basil Montagu whose son William and Dorothy had fostered for two years at Racedown in Dorset after the death of the boy's mother. 'Martha Ray was the mistress of the fourth Earl of Sandwich; she was shot by the Rev. James Hackman on April 7, 1779.'[12] It is difficult to imagine what psychological quirk drove Wordsworth to choose such an inappropriate name, but it would not be surprising if there was a link with his own obvious obsession with the deserted mother throughout the 1798 volume (most notably in 'The Female Vagrant' and 'The Forsaken Indian Woman'). The figure was common enough in the magazine poems, but the intensity of Wordsworth's treatment, and the haunting dreamlike sense of possible illusion in 'The Thorn', may reasonably be conjectured to derive partly from his guilt at having left his mistress Annette Vallon and baby daughter Caroline in France, the outbreak of war in 1793 thereafter making his return to marry Annette impossible.

So many obsessive concerns do not necessarily make a successful poem, and whether everything which went into this extraordinary experiment coalesces satisfactorily will be debated as long as Wordsworth is read. There is less disagreement about the other long ballad in the 1798 volume, 'The Idiot Boy', which is now generally recognised as an almost unqualified masterpiece. It has certain clearly defined objectives: psychological – to explore maternal affection in its purest form; social – to show how the mentally defective boy is accepted and cared for in a rural community; and spiritual – to penetrate into something of the idiot's secret life, which is 'hidden with God', as Wordsworth put it, borrowing St Paul's suggestive phrase for his own purpose in his letter replying to that generally enthusiastic appreciation of the *Lyrical Ballads* by the young John Wilson (Gill, pp. 620–5). Wilson had objected, as Coleridge was to do in the *Biographia Literaria*, that the disgust naturally associated with idiots and the 'excessive fondness' of his mother are likely to alienate the reader. Sensibilities have no doubt changed over the years, to some extent, but one can still appreciate Wordsworth's daring and estimate his achievement the more highly for it. The boldness lies in the way in which he emphasises the idiot's peculiarities of speech and his uncoordinated movements, as well as his mother's fussy fondness, and yet puts so much else into the poem that these features are taken up into the joyous whole. (He said that he 'never wrote anything with so much glee'.)[13] Although several features can be isolated for attention, it is the combined effect which tells.

The good humour is striking throughout. There is a strong mock-romance element, with echoes of Bürger's highly popular ballads, and largely playful references to the muses.[14] The narrator's involvement with the story as a concerned neighbour, doubtful about Betty's wisdom yet increasingly sympathetic, recalls Burns's narrative masterpiece 'Tam o' Shanter', published in 1791 but already classic. Some of the humour is associated with the horse: his thoughtfulness (122), and his near-overturning by Betty (385). Betty's actions are nearly always amusing, not least when she knocks the reluctant doctor up and totally forgets to mention poor Susan Gale. Susan's recovery is equally delightful. The humour in no way detracts from the sympathy, or the psychological realism, or the spirituality (like her son, Betty has a sort of hidden life: 'She sits, as if in Susan's face / Her life and soul were buried', 140–1); but it effectively keeps sentimentality at bay.

The poem is, as if in deliberate contrast to 'The Thorn', carefully plotted. Its topography is clearly delineated at the outset and adhered to throughout:

> And he must post without delay
> Across the bridge that's in the dale,

And by the church, and o'er the down,
To bring a doctor from the town,
Or she will die, old Susan Gale.

(52–6)

The progression of time between eight and five o'clock is
equally clearly delineated, often by the clock which is heard
striking eleven, twelve, one, and three (158, 162, 182, 281:
cf. 1, 456), and Wordsworth draws attention to his control
by ostentatiously framing his poem with owl hootings (3–6,
442–6), and by omitting the potentially tedious (214–16).

As in 'Goody Blake' the rhyme is cunningly handled as an
integral part of the effect. Betty Foy (could there be a
suggestion of *foi*, 'faith', in the name?) rhymes of course
with 'boy', but also with 'joy', and this is a supremely joyful
poem. Lines based on 'Him who you love, your idiot boy'
(11) form a sort of refrain (16, 51), and Wordsworth
emphasises Johnny's proud joy as he burrs and sits
awkwardly (19, 84–6), and Betty's as she watches her son
aloft (98). One is thus prepared for the *feu de joie* of the
reunion between mother and child at lines 368 onwards
with their repeated 'Foy' : 'boy' : 'joy' rhyming. Although
feminine rhymes are not used systematically as in 'Goody
Blake' and 'Simon Lee', there are some notable examples. A
pony must have 'bridle' and 'saddle', and these suggest the
word 'idle' (used in two different senses, the first unrhymed
but immediately following on 'With stirrup, saddle, or with
rein' at line 22; cf. 85) and 'fiddle-faddle' (14). A carefully
prepared feminine rhyme also occupies pride of place at the
end of the piece:

– Thus answered Johnny in his glory,
And that was all his travel's story.

(The preparatory appearance is at lines 133 and 136.)
'The Idiot Boy' is then a joyful, good-humoured, artful,
sympathetic poem. Yet Wordsworth also manages to give it
a quality of wonder and mystery. In this case the work had
its origin in an idiot's reported words which appear in the
verse as:

'The cocks did crow to-whoo, to-whoo,
And the sun did shine so cold.'[15]

29

That is 'defamiliarisation' with a vengeance – the idiot's or young child's freshness of vision, untrammelled by normal adult categories.[16] Its weird beauty has been prepared for by the hint of a frozen night spectacle at Johnny's setting-out:

> And while the pony moves his legs,
> In Johnny's left-hand you may see,
> The green bough's motionless and dead;
> The moon that shines above his head
> Is not more still and mute than he.
>
> (87–91)

In both cases the moon is central, and the moonlit landscape is presented with a magically intense quality which re-appears in the works of the artist Samuel Palmer a generation later:

> 'Tis silence all on every side;
> The town so long, the town so wide,
> Is silent as the skies.
>
> (254–6)

> She listens, but she cannot hear
> The foot of horse, the voice of man;
> The streams with softest sound are flowing
> The grass you almost hear it growing,
> You hear it now if e'er you can.
>
> (292–6)

There are many details of this intensely imagined kind in the poem for readers to discover on repeated readings, and they halo its holy fool with an enchanted glory which is yet firmly grounded in the thoughts and speech of everyday folk.

Two lyrics: 'It is the first mild day of March' and 'Lines Written in Early Spring'

In the ballads Wordsworth uses rudimentary language and forms with great sophistication. In the lyrics published in the 1798 volume the sophistication is still more apparent, though it never violates the essential simplicity which characterises most of the collection.

'Lines Written at a Small Distance from my House, and sent by my little Boy to the Person to whom they are addressed' is not an attractive title (it later became 'To My Sister'), but its prosaic literalness grounds the poem firmly in a particular setting and domestic situation (the 'Person' is Dorothy Wordsworth, and the boy young Basil Montagu, Martha Ray's grandson), and the first stanza shines out in radiant contrast:

> It is the first mild day of March:
> Each moment sweeter than before,
> The red-breast sings from the tall larch
> That stands beside our door.

The rhythm of the opening line is subtly poised, swinging gently on the accented off-beat 'mild'. In the third line the diction is crisp on the tongue, the rhythm again varied, and the red-breast and tall larch standing out cleanly. The freshness and exhilaration of this poem are to be achieved in part by such scrupulosity of diction and rhythmic flexibility.

The first chapter noted the way in which the progression of adjectives in the second stanza ('bare . . . bare . . . green') makes each of them emerge freshly. The stanza also introduces the concept, by which both Coleridge and Wordsworth were much attracted at the period, of the interconnecting cooperation of the natural elements, encapsulated here in the word 'yield':

> There is a blessing in the air,
> Which seems a sense of joy to yield
> To the bare trees, and mountains bare,
> And grass in the green field.

This natural yielding prompts the desired human response two stanzas later: 'this one day / We'll give to idleness'. Wordsworth's message to Dorothy is to leave her morning task and 'Come forth and feel the sun'. The word 'feel', in that cliché, turns out to be crucial as the poem develops, for this is 'the hour of feeling' (24), and such an hour, such a moment (the language is playfully exaggerated), 'may give us more / Than fifty years of reason' (25-6). The poem praises an instinctive joining in the unity of the one natural life, in which all participate, over dutiful observation of 'joyless forms' and carrying out of morning tasks, yet its cautious language denies any extremist anti-rationalism. It is 'one day' only that is to be given to idleness (and on it Wordsworth is already writing a poem!).[17] One moment 'may give us more / Than fifty years of reason': the force of that 'may' is uncertain, and it is not necessarily the same force as it exerts in the following stanza, 'Some silent laws our hearts may make', where it is reinforced by 'shall' in the next line. The reader's sensitivity to such verbal ambiguities has already been alerted in the second stanza, and it is further stimulated by a series of puns or plays on words. The 'joyless forms' which will not regulate this 'living Calendar' may be 'prescribed methods', or specifically 'written codes' (the modern sense of a form to be filled in appears to be a Victorian development). The 'spirit' of the season is drunk in at every pore by 'Our minds', where the sense of spirit as liquor is strong, with overtones of 'breath' and the more abstract sense also present. (This combination of abstract and physical is to be important in *The Prelude*.) In the following stanza the 'temper' which is to be taken from the year to come appears at first sight an abstract word: 'mental balance or composure', 'mental constitution', 'habitual disposition', 'temperament', and 'frame of mind' are some of the areas of significance listed in the *Oxford English Dictionary*. But 'temperament' is also a musical term, meaning 'tuning', and Wordsworth draws on this significance in the following stanza:

> We'll frame the measure of our souls,
> They shall be tuned to love.

'Tuned' is obviously musical, the tuning of an instrument, and 'measure' has several musical meanings, most commonly as another word for 'bar', but it also includes dance, melody, musical time in general, and rhythm. Moreover, 'measure' can mean poetic metre, and there is a host of possible non-musical significances which would be appropriate: size, criterion or standard (referring back to 'forms'), proportion or symmetry, moderation (temperance), completeness. There are also richnesses to be explored in 'frame', but it should by now be clear just how carefully Wordsworth has chosen his words, giving them room to expand to challenge the reader to fresh encounters on each perusal.

The oneness of life is reinforced by an ambiguity in the sixth stanza:

> Love, now an universal birth,
> From heart to heart is stealing,
> From earth to man, from man to earth . . . .

At first one thinks that love steals from human heart to human heart, perhaps specifically from Wordsworth's to Dorothy's, but the next line suggests a different reading – from Nature's heart to man's and back again. It is in the service of this love that Dorothy is asked to put on her 'woodland dress' (14) and become a spirit of the groves.

The poem is by way of being a New Year resolution. Wordsworth is assuming the freedom to rewrite the calendar which French revolutionaries had used spectacularly, but in this case the rewriting is a personal one as the 'living' calendar is begun in a sacred renewal:

> We from to-day, my friend, will date
> The opening of the year.

This is done in the service not of reason but of feeling.[18]

The companion lyric with the neutral but more manageable title 'Lines written in Early Spring' is a little less rich, but it is very tightly organised, not least by the soft consonants which dominate (*f/v*, *p/b*, *th*) and help to give it its gentleness. The theme of the one life[19] is again central: it is called a 'creed' in the last stanza, formalising the 'faith' in line 11, but Wordsworth admits that he cannot measure the buds' thoughts. (Thoughts are not purely rational in Wordsworth, but often arise from those moods of the mind (l. 3) which are to feature prominently in the 1807 *Poems*.) He can only say that 'the least motion which they made, / It seemed a thrill of pleasure'. This hesitancy is at its most striking in the penultimate stanza. Wordsworth is sceptical about the universality of pleasure (though some scientific opinion supported him),[20] but he 'must think, do all I can, / That there was pleasure there'. It is the intensity of his experience of the late onset of the 1798 spring that forms the basis of his faith, his creed: he cannot prevent these 'thoughts' (21). Cunningly and tellingly he plays with rationality to end his poem, as in the companion lyric, with a refrain-like repetition to signal closure, but here giving a dying fall:

> Have I not reason to lament
> What man has made of man?

Two dialogues: 'Anecdote for Fathers' and 'We are Seven'

Of all the poems in the first volume of *Lyrical Ballads* the two dialogues between adult and child will for many readers be the most disturbing. Both of them centre on the gulf between the adult's way of seeing the world (and talking about it) and the child's, a topic which was to become the subject of much of Wordsworth's finest poetry.

'Anecdote for Fathers, shewing how the art of lying may be taught' is a bald poem, of an extreme simplicity appropriate both to an adult–child exchange in general, and to the adult's remorseless pressure on the child in this particular case. Its baldness clearly disconcerted the older Wordsworth, and in 1827 he filled in some of the gaps with explanatory comments. Thus in lines 13–14 ('A day it was when I could bear / To think, and think, and think again') the second line became 'Some fond regrets to entertain', and line 54 ('And thus to me he made reply') became 'And eased his mind with this reply'. (The alteration of line 41 to read 'For here are woods, hills smooth and warm' to eliminate a double use of 'green' is probably an improvement.) In 1827 also, Wordsworth inserted some pretty, natural description before the dialogue. These changes alert the reader to the aggressive starkness of the poem in its original form.

Wordsworth makes it clear that the adult is using the boy to satisfy his own psychological needs. The boy is pretty, and the adult feels satisfaction in being loved by him: in his idleness the adult remembers his domicile a year earlier (which is almost an eternity for a child of five) and asks a comparative question which has no significance for a child, living in the present, and, in one sense, out of time.

Wordsworth suggests the adult's pressuring of the boy by allowing the rhyme to stick on 'arm'/'farm': the boy is held physically while the question is put, first in a neutral form, then (twice) implying the answer 'Kilve' with its 'delightful shore', its 'smooth shore by the green sea'. The boy naturally responds as the adult appears to wish him to, and is rewarded by an even more difficult supplementary question asking the reason, no less than five times (three was to seem enough in 1827, but in 1798 Wordsworth wanted to emphasise that this question is both more difficult and even less appropriate). What is more, the adult now stresses the 'woods and green-hills warm', so that the 'green sea' at Kilve begins to sound decidedly uninviting (41–4). The immediate desperate answer suggested by the weather-cock puts an end to the conversation.[21] One feels that the adult should apologise for his idly manipulative behaviour. Perhaps in a sense he does so at the end of the poem, to the reader, acknowledging that the child has much to teach the adult, as the tone changes with the disappearance of the remorselessly dinning 'Kilve'/'Liswyn' opposition.

This effective adult–child dialogue formula is repeated in 'We are Seven', an intensely serious poem in one respect, and yet one with a strong tendency to the ludicrous. Wordsworth allowed Coleridge to open it with a domestic joke. He told Isabella Fenwick how this came about:

> My friends will not deem it too trifling to relate that while walking to and fro I composed the last stanza first, having begun with the last line. When it was all but finished, I came in and recited it to Mr. Coleridge and my Sister, and said, 'A prefatory stanza must be added, and I should sit down to our little tea-meal with greater pleasure if my task were finished.' I mentioned in substance what I wished to be expressed, and Coleridge immediately threw off the stanza thus:
>
> 'A little child, dear brother Jem,' –
>
> I objected to the rhyme, 'dear brother Jem,' as being ludicrous, but we all enjoyed the joke of hitching-in our friend, James Tobin's name, who was familiarly called Jem.[22]

There is an appropriateness in the writer's domestic circle being brought into this poem, with its picture of the child's conception of a family circle as essentially unbroken by death.

The girl is (like Dorothy, and like 'Edward') something of a nature-spirit:

> She had a rustic, woodland air,
> And she was wildly clad.
>
> (9–10)

It is clear from her opening response that the dead siblings are closer to her even than the living in more than a merely physical sense, though Wordsworth takes care to ensure that the surviving relatives are physically elsewhere. Under the adult's amusingly obtuse, remorseless questioning the girl becomes more and more concrete: her sister and brother lie 'Beneath the church-yard tree', 'Their graves are green', and so on. The questioner's thinking remains abstract. The girl's matter-of-fact concreteness gives an unsentimentally moving force to her accounts of Jane's illness and death and of John's departure, besides suggesting the naturalness of the process of death by introducing the seasons. She recognises death in her own way, but denies that the dead don't count.[23]

The girl is aware of some basic religious concepts and has made 'God released her of her pain' her own, but she has not grasped the notion of Heaven, and as a result we are presented with an 'advanced' religious doctrine confronting and trying to beat down by repetition something approaching an animist primitivism. So, F.J. Hugo observes, her 'disarming co-operation with death throws him [the questioner] off-balance, because it evades both the repulsive and attractive sides of death and makes nonsense of the complexity of his feelings'.[24] In this case, unlike 'Anecdote for Fathers', the child defends her position and her mathematics in the face of adult pressure: she 'would have her will'. In contrast to the grotesquely comic adult, she maintains her status as a very dignified little girl.[25]

A blank verse meditation: 'Tintern Abbey'

'Tintern Abbey' (the accepted abbreviated title, though in one respect misleading, for the famous ruins play no overt part, has its dignified appropriateness) is Wordsworth's first unquestioned major published masterpiece, a rich, mature meditation. The full, noncommittal conventional topographical title once passed,[26] one is immediately made aware that this is to be an elevated, solemn piece:

> Five years have passed; five summers, with the length
> Of five long winters!

With this opening Wordsworth establishes the poem's characteristic movement, a steady pressing forward, heavily stressed, with a persistent use of probing quasi-improvisatory repetitions to explore the implications of central concepts. So the remainder of the opening paragraph is sustained by the word 'again', for at the core of the experience is Wordsworth's 'revisiting' a site: 'again . . . Once again . . . again . . . Once again'. In the second paragraph the word 'mood', crucial for the poem as for much of Wordsworth, is carefully defined and redefined – 'that blessed mood . . . that serene and blessed mood' – and allowed to echo on in some of the handful of rhymes or line-end assonances which his blank verse admits: 'blood . . . food . . . wood' (45, 65, 79). (The other important rhyme frames the final address to Dorothy, crucially preparing the ending: 'make'/'sake' at 122/160.) Wordsworth helps this quietly insistent forward movement by arranging his sentence endings in such a way that, before the conclusion, they only twice coincide with the end of a line (8, 58), and by ensuring that sentences do not regularly terminate at a fixed place in the line. More than half the sentences begin with conjunctions (four with 'Nor', three with 'And', two with 'Therefore' and 'For', and one with 'If'). The 'Nor's in particular, which dominate the final paragraph, are positive not negative, and echo the equally important 'more's which move the imagination forward. At the outset, in a curious but effective construction, Wordsworth observes:

> Once again
> Do I behold these steep and lofty cliffs,
> That on a wild secluded scene impress
> Thoughts of more deep seclusion; and connect
> The landscape with the quiet of the sky.

The effect is at once static, in the picturesque tradition of William Gilpin's tours, reinforced by the illogical but appropriate 'quiet', and expansive, as the imagination (literally the scene itself) is reminded by the cliffs of the deeper seclusion beyond them. Wordsworth has owed to the scene not only elevated feelings arising, as David Hartley had taught, from sense experience, and an impulse towards practical benevolence, but 'another gift, / Of aspect more sublime' (37–8). As he takes this theme up again at line 95 (he has felt 'a sense sublime / Of something far more deeply interfused') it is less clear to what point of comparison the word 'more' refers. Answers can be worked out (than 'The still, sad music of humanity' for instance), but the main function of the word is inseparable from the 'presence' sensed in the natural world. (The 'more' in the final line of the poem is similarly ambiguous if pressed.)[27]

Wordsworth acknowledges that this emotional expansiveness and steady progression as he is led on by Nature (71, 125; cf. 43) is not grounded in any intellectual certainty. 'Tintern Abbey' is a majestic poem, but it is conceptually a consciously evasive one. The crucial point comes at the end of the second paragraph, where he has reached a moment of apparent repose, though not quite at the end of a line:

> . . . we are laid asleep
> In body, and become a living soul:
> While with an eye made quiet by the power
> Of harmony, and the deep power of joy,
> We see into the life of things.

The lines are full of words ('power', 'joy', 'harmony', 'life') which Wordsworth was to employ again and again in the years ahead, here used in an attempt to grapple with the significance of the mood which he has described. But what follows is revealing:

> If this
> Be but a vain belief, yet, oh! how oft,
> In darkness, and amid the many shapes
> Of joyless day-light; when the fretful stir
> Unprofitable, and the fever of the world,
> Have hung upon the beatings of my heart,

38

> How oft, in spirit, have I turned to thee
> O sylvan Wye! Thou wanderer through the woods,
> How often has my spirit turned to thee!

The paragraph achieves full closure, but the possible vanity of the belief has not been argued away: Wordsworth has said that whatever the validity of the belief, his experience has been thus. Always in Wordsworth it is the experience which is defended to the uttermost: attempted understandings and explanations are often valuable in evaluating the experience, but ultimately they are expendable. Hence the poem's 'perhaps' (32), 'may' (37), 'dare to hope' (66), 'I would believe' (88), and 'perchance' (112, 147). Wordsworth is one of the most scrupulous investigators of feeling. In this case he has felt sensations in the blood and along the heart (28–9),[28] and has experienced 'feelings too / Of unremembered pleasure' (31–2). On his first visit in 1793, in his overwrought state of mind desperately seeking solace, the colours and forms of the natural world were 'a feeling and a love' (81), and he has since in calmer days 'felt / A presence' (94–5). It is this presence, thus felt, which in contrast to 'the hour / Of thoughtless youth' (90–1) 'disturbs' into thought, and towards belief. For when feeling and memory act in concert, as he was to put it in *The Prelude*, 'feeling comes in aid / Of feeling, and diversity of strength / Attends us, if but once we have been strong' (XI. 326–8).

II

Two elegiac poems: 'A slumber did my spirit seal' and 'The Two April Mornings'

The second volume of the *Lyrical Ballads*, dated 1800 but published in January 1801, has at its heart two groups of elegiac poems, one set concerned explicitly or by implication with the death of a young woman or girl, 'Lucy', the other with a dead schoolmaster, 'Matthew'. It seems likely that both these figures are composite creations, though there have been many speculations as to possible single originals. In neither of these groups does the narrator draw on the resources of the Christian faith. The consolation, in so far as it may be found, arises from remembering, from the naturalness of the setting, and (the main concern of this study) from aesthetic form.

In the Lucy poems ('Three years she grew', 'She dwelt among th'untrodden ways', 'A slumber did my spirit seal', and the later 'I travelled among unknown Men' published in 1807) the simplest words are placed so as to create an effect which is at once wholly original and apparently wholly inevitable:

>A slumber did my spirit seal;
>   I had no human fears:
>She seemed a thing that could not feel
>   The touch of earthly years.
>
>No motion has she now, no force;
>   She neither hears nor sees,
>Rolled round in earth's diurnal course
>   With rocks and stones and trees.

In one sense this is a miniature lyrical ballad, telling a story but in this case totally eliding the principal event. The narrator is presumably talking about a girl or young woman: the poem follows two Lucy lyrics in the 1800 volume. Her death is too painful to mention, but it is implied in the space between the stanzas. The passage of time is indicated by the simplest means, a change of tense, from past in the first stanza to present in the second. When Lucy was alive it seemed to the narrator that she would always be the same, immune to ageing. Now she is dead. Nothing could be simpler or more universally understandable than this.

The two stanzas of the poem are differentiated not only by tense, sense, and vocabulary, but by their whole sound. The first is gentle in its consonants (*sl*, *sp*, *h*, *f*, *th*, *t*); the second comes to be dominated by the forceful *rs*, which acquire an aural rolling from the occurrence in 'Rolled', and its accents are heavy: 'No motion', 'no force', 'Rolled round', the long *o* echoing on into 'stones'.

The choice and placing of the words seems inevitable, yet it is very curious. In the first stanza Lucy is presented as a spiritual being, a visitant, immune to 'The touch of earthly years', but the word 'spirit' refers not to her but to the narrator's consciousness: some of its force is transferred to her by courtesy. Similarly the narrator 'had no human fears'. This covers a variety of significances. He had no fears such as human beings usually have; such as, as a human being, he ought to have had; such as he would have had if Lucy had been human: he failed to recognise Lucy's humanity. Much depends on whether one is reading the poem for the first time (or imaginatively as if for the first time, an important discipline which is sometimes neglected), or allowing knowledge of the second stanza to cast an ironic light on the opening idealisings. The most striking transformation which occurs in the first stanza when it is read in the light of the second affects the word 'thing'. In the context of its own stanza this is a quietly tender use, as of a 'sweet little thing'. But since in the second stanza Lucy becomes a thing, a corpse, the retrospective irony is fearsome. No clearer example can be found in Wordsworth of a word having such different forces and significance as to be in effect two different words. A similar irony affects the word 'touch', a favourite Wordsworthian term for the gentleness of Nature. In his trancelike state the narrator thinks of even that ageing from which he imagines Lucy to be immune as no more than a 'touch'. By the time the second stanza has been absorbed, that 'touch' has become sinister.[29]

In comparison with the shifting terms of the first stanza and its latent ironies, the second is massively, even brutally, straightforward. Lucy is now part of a vast machine, and scientific words (or words with scientific resonance) come in: 'force' and 'diurnal'.[30] Logically, of course, Lucy is hardly more bound to the revolving motion of the earth dead than she had been when alive, but the contrast is between a spirit apparently immune to 'earthly years' and a corpse confined to a particular spot for ever, like inanimate boulders or rooted vegetation. She has no human 'force', in any of the rich varieties of possible significance, but is part of an inanimate play of physical forces, a world wholly concrete, where all that is distinctively human is made negative.

Every reader will be strongly affected by this poem, but it

is possible to react in very different ways; indeed, it is possible for a single reader to have more than one response. From one point of view it is a despairing utterance, from another a consolatory one. Lucy is dead, and that is the end. Or Lucy is dead, but she is a part of something majestic which transcends the merely human and the weak self-deceptiveness of the narrator before her death. When there is art of such quality present, a work can hardly be wholly negative. It has recognised a shape, and one might almost say with Samuel Beckett that it is the shape that matters. It has confronted death and the loss of illusion directly, with one sort of honesty, and has given that confrontation definitive expression. In eight lines, it has attained tragic status.

The Matthew poems ('If nature, for a favorite Child', 'The Two April Mornings', 'The Fountain', and the five elegies printed by Gill) deal with the death of one in the fullness of years, but his departure is still deeply disturbing, partly because of his erstwhile extreme liveliness: he was full of 'fun and madness' ('If nature', 22), a 'grey-haired Man of glee' ('The Fountain', 20). Although the poems employ religious terms – for example, 'Thou soul of God's best earthly mould' ('If nature', 29) – their feeling is again predominantly secular. Matthew's name on the school tablet is all that is left of him, and an extraordinary simile shocks the reader into an awareness of how much fun has disappeared from the community with Matthew's death:

> Poor Matthew, all his frolics o'er,
> Is silent as a standing pool,
> Far from the chimney's merry roar,
> And murmur of the village school.
>
> ('If nature', 17–20)

The most complex and rewarding of these poems, 'The Two April Mornings', involves not only Matthew's death (at the end) but a death akin to Lucy's, that of Matthew's daughter Emma. There is no better example in Wordsworth of the delicate balance in much of his work between cliché and originality, of the way in which the very ordinary is embraced and yet made to seem quite fresh.

The opening stanza alerts the reader to the conventionality

and originality which are to be blended in the poem as a whole:

> We walked along, while bright and red
> Uprose the morning sun,
> And Matthew stopped, he looked, and said,
> 'The will of God be done!'

The first two lines are unremarkable. The third begins with an illogical 'And', a device used by Wordsworth on several occasions: here one might have expected 'Till'. Matthew stops, he looks (at what?), and makes a pious exclamation whose import is unclear. The immediate effect is to arouse the reader's curiosity, but also to disconcert. The stanza which follows is straightforward, introducing into this poem that liveliness which is strongly emphasised in the companion pieces. The only possibly disconcerting note is the word 'glittering': encountered after reading 'If nature', this may be felt to echo the 'glittering gold' of the tablet. The third stanza stresses the carefree nature of the holiday jaunt, one word standing out by virtue of its precise observation, the 'steaming' rills.

The narrator enquires, on the reader's behalf as it were, about the significance of that remark of Matthew's in the fourth stanza, using a slightly jocular word, 'work', for the jaunt, and reminding the reader that idleness in Wordsworth can be a source of illumination beyond mere formal immersion in books. Matthew stops again, the progression freezes, and one is taken back by a trick of the memory to a similar stopping thirty years before:

> With rod and line my silent sport
> I plied by Derwent's wave,
> And, coming to the church, stopped short
> Beside my Daughter's grave.
>
> (29–32)

The word 'silent' changes its significance during the reading of the stanza. At first it is merely a description of angling, but by the time one reaches the end of the stanza Matthew's silence has acquired deeper undertones. The following stanza suggests an imagined speech heard much as it might have been spoken in such a situation. 'And then she sang!' is most telling: the force of the conjunction is equal to its naturalness, and the comparison with the nightingale is precisely the right poignant cliché, to be followed at once and brutally by another and very different well-worn phrase:

> Six feet in earth my Emma lay.

What follows is a fine example of the everyday transformed by emotion and by the poet's art:

> And, turning from her grave, I met
> Beside the church-yard Yew
> A blooming Girl, whose hair was wet
> With points of morning dew.
>
> A basket on her head she bare,
> Her brow was smooth and white,
> To see a Child so very fair,
> It was a pure delight!

There is no reason to suppose that this girl is imaginary, yet there is something quasi-visionary in these stanzas. In the first, it is the vividly perceived freshness, which is achieved by placing in the same position in successive lines words which are phonetically almost at opposite poles: 'blooming' and 'points'.[31] The 'points' stand out with extreme vividness, and since the rhymes in the poem have hitherto been unremarkable the 'Yew'/'dew' rhyme adds to the freshness. The second of these stanzas describing the girl is realistic, but at the same time statuesque in attitude and finish.

What happens next is extraordinary, one of the most expansive, cathartic comparisons in literature:

> No fountain from its rocky cave
> E'er tripped with foot so free,
> She seemed as happy as a wave
> That dances on the sea.

The sense of unfettered freedom, the hint of classical numen, the blending of human and natural, is striking, the more so since on its previous occurrence 'wave' rhymed with 'grave'. Matthew's response to this sight, '[I] did not wish her mine', is one of those utterances where the reader has to think carefully and explore its possible significance in the light of the poem as a whole. Matthew does not wish the girl to be his, perhaps, because he could not face the possibility of another loss, or because Emma is irreplaceable, or because in a sense Emma is complete and perfect in memory. Readers will have their own suggestions to make, arising from responsive contemplation of what has gone before.

To the levels of time already encountered, Wordsworth adds one more, bringing the reader imaginatively to the time of writing:

> Matthew is in his grave, yet now
> Methinks I see him stand,
> As at that moment, with his bough
> Of wilding in his hand.

Thus finally the whole experience is arrested permanently in memory, and in art. Wordsworth disrupts his readers' sense of time to take them out of time, to leave them with a perfection of eternal contemplation which is not divorced from human sorrow or human transience, but which transfigures it. The effect, though not specifically religious, is akin to that of such religious masterpieces as Piero della Francesca's *Baptism of Christ* in the National Gallery in London, or Stravinsky's *Symphony of Psalms*. The poem is a set of precarious and delicate balancings – of art and life, cliché and originality, sorrow and joy, movement and stasis, time and eternity.

A blank verse pastoral narrative: 'Michael'

Most of the 1800 volume was composed after Wordsworth's return to the Lake District at the end of 1799.[32] Its inscriptions and minor pastorals are the most obvious examples of a desire to colonise or repossess a landscape imaginatively; the long fragmentary poem 'Home at Grasmere', which remained largely unpublished during Wordsworth's lifetime, is a fascinating though often somewhat hyperbolic song of ecstatic celebration by the homecomer; but Wordsworth's deepest acts of repossession, of re-establishing connections, are to be found in the Matthew poems and 'Michael' (which here stands also for the other long pastoral 'The Brothers'). Crucial to the poet's thought from now on is the idea that death and suffering are more readily accepted in a rural environment than in the city. In 'The Brothers' the priest maintains that because of the constant remembrance of the departed, and of course because of Christian confidence,

> The thought of death sits easy on the man
> Who has been born and dies among the mountains;
>
> (179–80)

and in that celebratory poem 'Home at Grasmere' Wordsworth writes:

> . . . here may the heart
> Breathe in the air of fellow-suffering
> Dreadless, as in a kind of fresher breeze
> Of her own native element.
>
> (448–51)

Along with 'The Ruined Cottage', which was composed in 1797, not published as a separate poem but incorporated after revision in the first book of *The Excursion*, 'Michael' is the most consummate of Wordsworth's blank-verse narratives. It is a story of transparent simplicity and immediate emotional appeal, but full of subtleties for the alert reader.

There survives in manuscript part of a jocular ballad version of the story,[33] and traces of its robustness may be discerned in the very different poem published in 1800. The opening of the story proper, ignoring the introduction, could be described as jaunty:

> Upon the Forest-side in Grasmere Vale
> There dwelt a Shepherd, Michael was his name,
> An old man, stout of heart, and strong of limb.

But 'Michael' is predominantly a gentle, solemn poem, and, as the lines that follow those quoted confirm, its language is very scrupulous and new-minted: Michael's 'mind was keen, / Intense, and frugal, apt for all affairs' (44–5). The poem inherits from the lyrical ballads a refusal to dwell on the sensational aspect of the story: almost all of it is devoted to bringing out the characters' feelings, and the principal action is allotted only the perfunctory penultimate paragraph.

The introductory paragraph alerts the reader to some of the terms and concepts that are to dominate the main part of the poem, binding together Michael, the natural world, and a narrator who may in this case without distortion be identified with the poet. Its aim is to slow polite readers down, to withdraw them from the 'public way', to make them consider a character whom, like the unfinished sheepfold, they 'might pass by, / Might see and notice not' (15–16). The natural world is (like Michael, and like the poem) to be initially forbidding, but then surprisingly gentle:

> You will suppose that with an upright path
> Your feet must struggle; in such bold ascent
> The pastoral Mountains front you, face to face.
> But, courage! for beside that boisterous Brook
> The mountains have all opened out themselves,
> And made a hidden valley of their own.
>
> (3–8)

(The unusual syntax and initial vowels of 'all opened out themselves' reinforce the notion of generous yielding.) It is clear that one of the poet's main concerns is continuity. As a boy he had been 'led on' by his natural story to think 'On man; the heart of man, and human life' (33), and he sees the story as connecting himself with 'youthful Poets, who among these Hills / Will be my second self when I am gone' (38–9). Continuity is also Michael's overriding concern, as he recalls his parents who, in a potent phrase, 'were not loth / To give their bodies to the family mold' and wishes 'that thou should'st live the life they lived' (379–81). Although Michael has gone and his land has been sold, and although his type of smallholder (the Cumbrian 'statesman') is a threatened species, Wordsworth will ensure that the tradition is carried on in a new form. The fellow-feeling which the poet experiences for Michael is suggested in his allusion to his own early days when he loved the country folk

> not verily
> For their own sakes, but for the fields and hills
> Where was their occupation and abode.
>
> (24–6)

It would be going too far to maintain that Michael loves the land (or himself, given substance by the land), and Luke only for the sake of the land, but there is an element of truth in the proposition.

The introductory paragraph also alerts the reader to the bald nature of the story which is in the offing, 'ungarnished with events' (19), and Wordsworth, echoing Milton's 'fit audience though few', defines his readership as 'a few natural hearts' (36). If a person will read, it must be on those terms. One is withdrawn from vulgar literary expectations and prepared to feel for apparently unimportant things, which yet exemplify the most universal human feelings.

As is often the case ('Tintern Abbey' was noted as an example), Wordsworth's blank verse is not entirely un-rhymed, and the occasional rhyme or assonance is used to reinforce certain words and concepts, or to shape the paragraphs. This introductory paragraph is another excellent example. The stones of the unfinished sheepfold are the climax to which the work moves in the celebrated line 'And never lifted up a single stone' (475). Wordsworth evidently has this ending in mind and allows his initial paragraph to touch on the 'stone' rhyme. The word itself is plural at the end of line 17, but one is conscious of its link with lines 8 ('own'), 10 ('alone', conceptually reinforced by 'solitude' at the end of 13), and finally 39 ('gone').

In her journal entry for 11 October 1800 Dorothy Wordsworth describes a piece of field research which she undertook with her brother during the composition of 'Michael':

A fine October morning. Sat in the house working all the morning. Wm composing – Sally Ashburner learning to mark. After Dinner we walked up Greenhead Gill in search of a sheepfold. We went by Mr Ollif's and through his woods. It was a delightful day and the views looked excessively chearful and beautiful chiefly that from Mr Oliff's field where our house is to be built. The colours of the mountains soft and rich, with orange fern – the Cattle pasturing upon the hill-tops Kites sailing as in the sky above our heads – Sheep bleating and in lines and chains and patterns scattered over the mountains. They come down and feed on the little green

islands in the beds of the torrents and so may be swept away.
The Sheepfold is falling away it is built nearly in the form of
a heart unequally divided.

The heart form of the structure is nowhere mentioned in
'Michael'. It has been elided.[34] But in its place is the
richest set of uses of the word 'heart' in Wordsworth and
thus in English. From the opening exhortation 'But,
courage!' (cor-age), the taking of heart in a multiplicity of
shades of meaning is perceived to be at the core, or heart,
of the poem.

There are other words round which the poem pivots.
'Hope' enters later, but it is crucial, for without it life
fails.[35] Michael and his wife have 'objects and hopes'
(123), Luke is the source of 'hope' for Michael especially,
the bad news 'for a moment took / More hope out of his
life than he supposed / That any old man ever could have
lost' (228-30), and the suggested plan to avoid selling the
land is 'a cheerful hope' (253), a 'good hope' (288). After
nights of troubled sleep 'all [Michael's] hopes were gone'
(303), and the word occurs twice in his final speech to
Luke (399, 409). There is a fascinating complex of words
– 'love', 'land', 'Luke', 'loss', 'lose' – which echo
ambiguously through the poem. There is, too, the
repetition of that 'public way', which the reader was
invited to leave at the outset of the poem, when Luke sets
out on his ill-fated journey from the secluded vale (436),
yet the quiet domestic life is not entirely a private affair,
for the light becomes 'a public Symbol of the life, / The
thrifty Pair had lived' (137–8).

Wordsworth's handling of the blank verse in 'Michael'
has attracted much praise, generally of a somewhat vague
kind. The verse is subtle and varied, constantly
reinforcing in a delicate manner the sense and the gentle
but firm movement of the poem. A few examples out of
the many possible will illustrate something of the way in
which this is achieved. In the lines

> he had been alone
> Amid the heart of many thousand mists
> That came to him and left him on the heights
>
> (58–60)

the 'alone' at the end of the first line continues the emphasis initiated in the introductory paragraph. 'Amid' also takes up from the introduction the concept of an inner sanctum, and the whole line is of extraordinary originality and force: 'Amid the heart' is freshly conceived, as are so many phrases to do with the heart in this poem and elsewhere in Wordsworth, and one notes that all the mists have one heart, amid which Michael has been, alone. One may compare the way in which the concept is taken up towards the end of the poem, using the preposition 'among',

> Up to the heights, and in among the storms,
> Will I without thee go again, and do
> All works which I was wont to do alone,
> Before I knew thy face,
>
> (404–7)

and 'Among the rocks / He went' (464–5). Then, in line 60, how better to convey the shifting movement of the mists than by that soft alternation: 'came to him and left him'? One may also note the quiet onomatopoeic rhythm of lines 167–8, 'he had rocked / His cradle, as with a woman's gentle hand'; the pathetic effect of the deliberate rhythm and initial vowels in line 230, 'That any old man ever could have lost'; the rapid unstressed movement of lines 256–7, 'He shall possess it, free as is the wind / That passes over it'; the strange formality of the disyllabic 'kissèd him' in line 432; and the awkward but impressive 'still looked up upon the sun' in line 465, which was conventionalised in 1832 to read 'up towards the sun' and in 1836 to 'up to sun and cloud'.

Literary allusion plays a crucial role in the poem. Wordsworth greatly admired Burns's work, and the description of cottage life clearly recalls 'The Cotter's Saturday Night'. Compare

> . . . all
> Turned to their cleanly supper-board, and there
> Each with a mess of pottage and skimmed milk,
> Sate round their basket piled with oaten cakes,
> And their plain home-made cheese
>
> (100–4)

with these lines from Burns's poem:

> But now the Supper crowns their simple board,
>   The healsome *Porritch*, chief of SCOTIA'S food:
> The soupe their *only Hawkie* does afford,
>   That 'yont the hallan snugly chows her cood:
> The *Dame* brings forth, in complimental mood,
> To grace the lad, her weel-hain'd kebbuck, fell;
>   And aft he's prest, and aft he ca's it guid;
>   The frugal *Wifie*, garrulous, will tell,
> How 'twas a towmond auld, sin' Lint was i' the bell.
>
> The chearfu' Supper done, wi' serious face,
>   They, round the ingle, form a circle wide.
>
>   (91–101)

No doubt one is meant to assume that the Cumbrian family are as devout as Burns's circle gathered for domestic worship, and it is likely also that Burns's fourteenth stanza helped to suggest Wordsworth's patriarchal scene between father and son at the sheepfold. Burns writes:

> The priest-like Father reads the sacred page,
>   How *Abram* was the Friend of GOD on high.
>
>   (118–19)

The laying of the corner-stone in Wordsworth is a 'covenant', and the reference is unmistakably to the several stones set up in the Old Testament as witnesses of compacts between man and man, or God and Israel, of which the most relevant is that at the end of Joshua (24: 25–7):

> So Joshua made a covenant with the people that day, and set them a statute and an ordinance in Shechem.
>   And Joshua wrote these words in the book of the law of God, and took a great stone, and set it up there under an oak, that was by the sanctuary of the Lord.
>   And Joshua said unto all the people, Behold, this stone shall be a witness unto us; for it hath heard all the words of the Lord which he spake unto us: it shall be therefore a witness unto you, lest ye deny your God.

The unease which some readers feel in Michael's presence, and their doubts about his treatment of his son, arise partly

51

from this severe Old Testament background, and they may be further strengthened by the gently ironic echo of the parable of the Prodigal Son earlier in the poem:

> – Make ready Luke's best garments, of the best
> Buy for him more.

(289–90)

Compare

> But the father said to his servants, Bring forth the best robe,
> and put it on him; and put a ring on his hand, and shoes on
> his feet:
>> And bring hither the fatted calf, and kill it. (Luke 15: 22–3)

The parable is of course reversed, for this is a departure, and there is to be no happy ending. It would not be surprising if Luke's name had its origin in a probably subconscious recollection of the parable which the poem may be seen as inverting.[36] None of this is to deny Michael's predominant admirable qualities, but the undertones in his character are ambiguous and are handled with fine delicacy, a characteristic fundamental to this very great poem's art.

CHAPTER 3

The Prelude
(1805)

I

Among Coleridge's many unfulfilled plans was one for a major philosophical poem to be entitled *The Brook*. He envisaged that this work would occupy him for twenty years: 'I should not think of devoting less than 20 years to an Epic Poem. Ten to collect materials and warm my mind with universal science . . . the next five to the composition of the poem – and the five last to the correction of it.'[1] In the case of *The Prelude*, which was written by way of preparation for Wordsworth's unfinished philosophical poem *The Recluse* (to which 'Home at Grasmere' and *The Excursion* belong), Coleridge's plan might be paraphrased thus: 'Thirty years to the collection of materials, seven to the composition, and forty-five to the correction of it.' The subject of the poem is 'the formation of my own mind' as Wordsworth said in 1839,[2] so that its materials extend from the poet's earliest childhood to (and indeed throughout) the years of composition. Its actual writing began in a fragmentary manner during 1798, and it coalesced into a rough two-book draft in the following year; composition continued unevenly until five books (not altogether identical with Books I to V of 1805) were complete in March 1804, and was then immediately resumed to result in the thirteen-book version of 1805. At various stages in later life Wordsworth returned to his unpublished poem to revise it extensively in detail, and it was finally published shortly after his death in 1850.

Dr Johnson said of *Paradise Lost* that no man ever wished it longer, and the same is no doubt true of *The Prelude,* one of the very few poems in English which can challenge comparison with Milton's masterpiece. Wordsworth himself thought it 'an alarming length'.[3] The 1850 version has the advantage of being substantially shorter than that of 1805. Among its other virtues, many of which were well summed up by Ernest de Selincourt in the introduction to his pioneering parallel text edition, the most notable is a general tendency to tighten up and prune loose and diffuse expressions.[4] Whereas most of Wordsworth's revisions of his shorter poems are deleterious, there is a good deal to be said in favour of some of his alterations to the 1805 *Prelude,* and the reader is urged not to lose sight of 1850, since a comparison of the two versions can often be a fascinating and instructive exercise in poetic craftsmanship. Nevertheless this chapter addresses itself primarily to the 1805 text, not merely for the sake of consistency or because it alone is included in the Oxford Authors edition, but because the present writer is one of those who believe that when all the arguments in favour of 1850 have been carefully considered, and their local validity sometimes accepted, 1805 is the more vital, daring work. As so often William Empson goes to the heart of the matter:

> In general, I agree with a recent defender of the older man
> (M.E. Burton *One Wordsworth*) who says that he did not try
> to hide his early political and religious opinions any further
> when he re-wrote, indeed, he sometimes enlarged upon a
> vaguely unorthodox idea such as the world-soul; he was
> merely 'improving the style'. But this improvement, which
> was mainly a process of packing the lines more fully, meant
> invoking Milton and his sense of the unrelaxing Will; whereas
> the whole point and delicacy of the first version was to
> represent a wavering and untrammelled natural growth. The
> improvement was, therefore, about the most destructive
> thing he could have done, far worse than changing the
> supposed opinions.[5]

It is worth putting up with a good deal of roughness and occasional verbosity and conceptual vagueness for the sake of the 1805 *Prelude*'s freshness, its superior poetic movement, and its closeness to felt experience. (1850's most notable and successful deletion, of the exceedingly dull tale of Vaudracour and Julia – introduced at the end of the ninth book as a heavily disguised personal allusion to Wordsworth's affair with Annette Vallon during his second visit to France in 1791–92 – can easily be made by readers of 1805 for themselves.)

Like most poems of the Romantic period and since, *The Prelude* is *sui generis*, a unique mixture of kinds. Its allusions to *Paradise Lost* claim for it something of epic status, with conscious audacity ('a thing unprecedented in Literary history that a man should talk so much about himself', said Wordsworth),[6] but it is clearly not an epic in any traditional sense. A.C. Bradley pointed out that its basic impulse is lyrical, and one might think of it as a lyrical epic to follow on from the 'lyrical ballads'.[7] Since the poem is addressed throughout to Coleridge, it can be regarded as a gigantic specimen of the 'conversation poem' form which Coleridge had made very much his own in works such as 'Frost at Midnight', 'This Lime-Tree Bower My Prison', or the verse letter to Sara Hutchinson. There are also strong Juvenalian satirical elements in the descriptions of Cambridge and London, and the progress through loss and dislocation to restoration and wholeness resembles that of romance.

The principles governing the poem's structure are not immediately obvious. Milton planned *Paradise Lost* architectonically, like a great building, so that its twelve-book form (itself an epic imitation of Virgil) makes sense when considered as four groups of three books, three of four, six of two, or two of six – to mention only the simpler divisions and ignoring the underlying five-act tragedy of the original, almost identical, ten-book poem. That is an amazing feat of baroque engineering, on a par with Wren's contemporary St Paul's Cathedral. The 1805 *Prelude*, though, is in thirteen books, which cannot be divided mathematically, and it was clearly not planned: it evolved, though of course many conscious decisions were made during its progress as to the disposition of materials. The resulting structure is somewhat puzzling on first acquaintance, but it makes sense, and it is for the most part a really satisfying organic whole: it is significant that in spite of innumerable detailed alterations 1850 preserved 1805's structure essentially unchanged.

The Prelude's structure may usefully be approached by way of several of its dominant images.[8] In a fine essay G. Wilson Knight has indicated something of the way in which the surface on which the poet walks is borne up, sustained by great reserves of energy and power.[9] This energy is suggested by a number of words beginning with the prefix 'under-', some of them coined by Wordsworth. When he read inferior books his 'under soul' – his inner imaginative self, the deepest region of his subconscious – was 'hushed' and 'locked up', as it were out of use for the time being (III, 539–40); before the crossing of the Alps in Book VI he experienced an 'under-thirst' of his deepest being for something more satisfying than the superficial enjoyment which the scenery had thitherto afforded him (VI, 489); and among those countrymen who in the poet's estimation lead deep but silent lives 'Words are but under-agents in their souls' (XII, 272): that is to say that the words are not available because of lack of education, but the ideas which the words represent are there, deep down within them.

Frequently the earth as it is usually apprehended seems merely a dream, absorbed by the mind or passing like insubstantial forms, as in the tired walk before the meeting with the discharged soldier (IV, 392ff). In such visionary moments unknown modes of being are sensed. Thus in Wordsworth's description of the after-effects of his stealing of the skiff the word 'Forms' recurs with tremendous power:

> . . . after I had seen
> That spectacle, for many days, my brain
> Worked with a dim and undetermined sense
> Of unknown modes of being; in my thoughts
> There was a darkness, call it solitude,
> Or blank desertion, no familiar shapes
> Of hourly objects, images of trees,
> Of sea or sky, no colours of green fields;
> But huge and mighty Forms that do not live
> Like living men moved slowly through my mind
> By day and were the trouble of my dreams.
>
> (417–27)

That is the darkness beneath the earth, the sense of mystery at the heart of things, when the comforting colours disappear, leaving the monochrome of dreams that are often close to nightmare. 'Trouble' is one of Wordsworth's powerful terms, indicating subdued and ominous agitation.[10] The surface of the earth becomes unstable, and solitary objects are portrayed in such a way that there is something haunting about their 'forms', as there had often been in the *Lyrical Ballads*. So, the shepherd and his dogs appear in Book VIII:

> Girt round with mists they stood and looked about
> From that enclosure small, inhabitants
> Of an aerial Island floating on,
> As seemed, with that Abode in which they were,
> A little pendant area of grey rocks,
> By the soft wind breathed forward.
>
> (VIII, 96–101)

Such quasi-supernatural visions produce in the poet a sense of unease, and this is greatest in the extraordinary meeting with the discharged soldier. The poet is tired, and his first sight of the figure is of something utterly strange and other:

> He was of stature tall,
> A foot above man's common measure tall,
> Stiff in his form, and upright, lank and lean;
> A man more meagre, as it seemed to me,
> Was never seen abroad by night or day.
> His arms were long, and bare his hands; his mouth
> Shewed ghastly in the moonlight.
>
> (IV, 405–11)

The word 'ghastly' occurs again in the scene where the body of the drowned man is dragged up from beneath the smooth surface of the delightful lake at Esthwaite. These are both disquieting scenes which nevertheless result in a great calm when they have been reflected on. The soldier's moaning, his lack of any overt emotion, and his haunting final words spoken with 'ghastly mildness' have led D.G. James to think of Keats's Moneta, the deathlike figure at the centre of the revised *Hyperion* fragment.[11] The apprehension common to all these passages is summed up in Wordworth's argument, extant in one manuscript only, for sparing the monastery at Grande Chartreuse: it should be allowed to remain because it is

> this embodied dream
> This substance by which mortal men have clothed,
> Humanly clothed, the ghostliness of things
> In silence visible and perpetual calm.[12]

Wordsworth is sometimes accused of undue and unwarranted optimism, but his vision is a stern one; even if its end is joy and love, his universe frequently works by means of pain, terror, and dereliction. More than one reader has been put in mind of Gerard Manley Hopkins's 'terrible' sonnets:

> O the mind, mind has mountains; cliffs of fall
> Frightful, sheer, no-man-fathomed. Hold them cheap
> May who ne'er hung there.[13]

The structure of *The Prelude* is governed by this fundamental vision, which has been called 'apocalyptic', and it can be viewed, as can many aspects of this work, as a development from the *Lyrical Ballads*. In 'The Two April Mornings' the complex time levels suggested a spiritual apprehension of non-time, and the spatial expansions implied great reserves of vitality. The structure of *The Prelude* is based on a similar juggling with time and space, with a strong contrast between horizontal and vertical images. The poem moves forward with an energy derived partly from the sweeping blank verse paragraphs, partly from characteristic recurrent images of travelling and voyaging, of roads stretching into infinity, of an inspiriting breeze, above all of flowing water. But frequently in 'spots of time' (or what Joyce was to call 'epiphanies') the surface breaks, the ice cracks, shafts are sunk into the visionary depths of the earth, into the mind's abyss, into the past, revealing those sometimes terrifying energies upon which the fabric of the world of experience is borne up. Two whole books, the retrospective books, emphasise the vertical probing as Wordsworth investigates the foundations of the precarious platform on which he is standing. In an unpublished fragment he wrote:

> I look into past times as prophets look
> Into futurity, a [?] of life runs back
> Into dead years.[14]

There are two images which stand out above all others in this connection. The first illustrates that complex interaction of past and present which Wordsworth outlined in the Preface to *Lyrical Ballads*, and it may be seen as imaging one of the fundamental structural principles of the whole poem:

> As one who hangs down-bending from the side
> Of a slow-moving Boat, upon the breast
> Of a still water, solacing himself
> With such discoveries as his eye can make,
> Beneath him, in the bottom of the deeps,
> Sees many beauteous sights, weeds, fishes, flowers,
> Grots, pebbles, roots of trees, and fancies more,
> Yet often is perplexed, and cannot part
> The shadow from the substance, rocks and sky,
> Mountains and clouds, from that which is indeed
> The region, and the things which there abide
> In their true dwelling; now is crossed by gleam
> Of his own image, by a sunbeam now,
> And motions that are sent he knows not whence,
> Impediments that make his task more sweet;
> – Such pleasant office have we long pursued
> Incumbent o'er the surface of past time
> With like success.
>
> (IV, 247–64)

Past and present are inextricably entangled there, as in the process of composition, and the entire process is given added life by gracious inexplicable inspirations and enlightenments. One may link with this the final image of the poem, the vision on Snowdon, in which the greatest of all Romantic abysses (greater even than that in Coleridge's 'Kubla Khan') emblems the bursting forth from the depths of the terrible but all-sustaining power of the human imagination itself:

> . . . we stood, the mist
> Touching our very feet; and from the shore
> At distance not the third part of a mile

Was a blue chasm; a fracture in the vapour,
A deep and gloomy breathing-place, through which
Mounted the roar of waters, torrents, streams
Innumerable, roaring with one voice.
The universal spectacle throughout
Was shaped for admiration and delight,
Grand in itself alone, but in that breach
Through which the homeless voice of waters rose,
That dark deep thoroughfare, had Nature lodged
The Soul, the Imagination of the whole.

(XIII, 53–65)

Associated with this fundamental horizontal-vertical structural principle is the constant interplay between the experiences being recalled and the poet's concerns at the time of composition. Shortly before beginning work on what was to become *The Prelude*, Wordsworth read Sterne's novel *Tristram Shandy*. It may seem perverse to suggest a connection between two such apparently diametrically opposed works, but in a lecture given in 1818 Coleridge was to have brilliantly appreciative things to say about Sterne's handling of time past and time present in that novel, and it may be conjectured that Wordsworth's great structure takes Sterne's seminal work as one of its points of departure.[15] Like Tristram, Wordsworth is struggling against impossible odds, in his case to capture a fading and potentially restorable and restorative vision, with declining powers:

The days gone by
Come back upon me from the dawn almost
Of life: the hiding-places of my power
Seem open; I approach, and then they close;
I see by glimpses now; when age comes on,
May scarcely see at all, and I would give,
While yet we may, as far as words can give,
A substance and a life to what I feel:
I would enshrine the spirit of the past
For future restoration.

(XI, 334–43)

One is always conscious that the writer's circumstances are changing and his ideas developing as he tells the story of the growth of his mind, and although the later revisions attempt to render the work more monolithic and less fluid they are in one sense the final stages of a continuing process.[16]

The invocations to Coleridge, usually addressed as 'Friend', which punctuate the poem are further reminders of human mutability, as the history of his past and present life is sketched in parallel to Wordsworth's. They also have an important local structural function, ending several books firmly. Within books, Coleridge's appearance often indicates an important transitional moment, though there can be other reasons for invoking him, such as the two poets' shared experience of out-of-the-way reading (V, 233) or a desire to have him present, as it were, at moments of exceptional confessional frankness or tenderness. Several of these appearances will be noted in the following analysis which, bearing these general structural principles in mind, seeks to isolate the main movements of this unique organism. It takes as its main subject the poem as first completed in 1805, and largely ignores its earlier evolution. The analysis is offered by way of suggestion only, in the hope that readers may find it helpful as a guide or a stimulation. Each person will of course see the structure differently, and some will see it very differently from the present writer: that is to be welcomed, and indeed the poem can change its shape in a fascinating way on repeated readings. For some, it will make less sense than this analysis suggests: that does not mean that their own readings are inferior or less valid, though equally it should not be held to guarantee that they are more profound.[17]

II

Books I to V, being in most essentials the poem as conceived in 1804, consist of an introduction and narrative (I–IV), and a supplement (V) isolating for special treatment the subject of books which the narrative has neglected in its concentration on the poet and in relation to nature and his fellow-men.

Book I, 'Introduction: Childhood and School-time', has three main sections (1–271, 271–501, and 501–end). The first section moves from initial elation to doubt. The opening exordium (1–54) has complex origins, but in its present context it reads as a hymn of gratitude on the poet's release from city life, expressing his eager expectation of a period of creativity at Grasmere. As Wordsworth explains to Coleridge (55–67) this is a rare example of a spontaneous effusion. Its transcription here is designed partly to begin the poem with a burst of energy, partly to indicate that the bulk of the work will not be like this but will take the form of an intricate blend of past and present, and partly to imply that in comparison with this initial fluency what follows is going to be considerably more difficult to achieve. For as the wind-harp ceases to sound (104–7) it is made clear, at first very gently, that this is to be in part one of those Romantic poems about the writing of poetry, indeed about the difficulty – almost the impossibility – of writing poetry. Now, as Wordsworth writes, as the tenses change from present to past, it becomes apparent that his plan to earth his imaginative energies in Grasmere, to find sufficient scope for them in that peculiar nook, has run into difficulties (127–41). As he talks to Coleridge about the mind at once calm and goaded (his image of the dove echoing that of the brooding Spirit of God at the Creation) one may be reminded a little of Samuel Beckett's celebrated expression of his artistic dilemma: 'The expression that there is nothing to express, nothing with which to express, nothing from which to express, no power to express, no desire to express, together with the obligation to express.'[18] Coleridge has urged his friend on to a major work, a philosophical poem to rival *Paradise Lost*, but Wordsworth is not in the mood, is not inspired. With such high self-consciousness predominating, it is appropriate that he should proceed (157–251) to imitate Milton's secondary epic listing of rejected subjects at the beginning of Book IX of *Paradise Lost*. This passage is partly, like the whole poem indeed in one sense, a sublime marking of time, vamping till ready. It is also an indication that, just as Milton deliberately transformed the classical heroic epic tradition in the interests of a Christian heroism of 'patience and heroic martyrdom', so Wordsworth is preparing his own radical transformation of the long poem towards a yet gentler mode, 'Some Tale from my own heart' (221) or

> some philosophic Song
> Of Truth that cherishes our daily life;
> With meditations passionate from deep
> Recesses in man's heart.
>
> (230–3)

If this 'more philosophic song' is the projected *Recluse*, the 'Tale from my own heart' is not far removed from *The Prelude* as it develops and as he characterises it in Book III, with another echo of the passage in Milton:

> O Heavens! how awful is the might of Souls,
> And what they do within themselves, while yet
> The yoke of earth is new to them, the world
> Nothing but a wild field where they were sown.
> This is, in truth, heroic argument,
> And genuine prowess, which I wished to touch
> With hand however weak.
>
> (III, 178–84)

The first section of the book ends in near-despair with another Miltonic echo as Wordsworth accuses himself of cowardice and selfishness, 'Unprofitably travelling towards the grave, / Like a false steward who hath much received / And renders nothing back' (269–71), the reference being to Milton's own bleak allusion to the parable of the talents in his sonnet 'On His Blindness'.

It is possible at this point for Wordsworth to lead quite naturally into the 'Was it for this?' opening of the 1799 two-book *Prelude* fragment, which now forms the second section of 1805's opening book (271–501) and gives the appearance of shaking off paralysis as the poet introduces a series of vivid vignettes from his childhood brought to mind by the reiterated question. A useful key to the structure at this stage is a concept which is to govern many later passages, and indeed much of Wordsworth's poetry from this period onwards. Nature is conceived as having acted on the young poet by means of beauty and fear, by *ethos* and *pathos*:[19] both the beauty of the Derwent at Cockermouth and the fear of the woodcock stealing or the skiff episode are educative for the future visionary poet, and the end result of the double excitation is that profound but not empty calm which

63

Wordsworth often seems to have desired above all else:

> The mind of Man is framed even like the breath
> And harmony of music. There is a dark
> Invisible workmanship that reconciles
> Discordant elements, and makes them move
> In one society. Ah me! that all
> The terrors, all the early miseries,
> Regrets, vexations, lassitudes, that all
> The thoughts and feelings which have been infused
> Into my mind, should ever have made up
> The calm existence that is mine when I
> Am worthy of myself! Praise to the end!
> Thanks likewise for the means! But I believe
> That Nature, oftentimes, when she would frame
> A favored Being, from his earliest dawn
> Of infancy doth open out the clouds,
> As at the touch of lightning, seeking him
> With gentlest visitation; not the less,
> Though haply aiming at the self-same end,
> Does it delight her sometimes to employ
> Severer interventions, ministry
> More palpable, and so she dealt with me.
>
> (351–71)

It should be stressed – for it is fundamental to an appreciative reading of the poem – that Wordsworth's meditations are, at their best as here, no less alert and vigorous imaginatively and verbally than the descriptive vignettes which they accompany.[20]

The imaginative power and exuberance of this second section with its specific 'spots of time', as they are to be called later, is succeeded in the final section (501–end) by a more general survey of the same period concentrating on plain homely amusements during which the *pathos* is relegated to an outer darkness (525–70), and on calmer and subtler pleasures (571–608). In a characteristically scrupulous analysis of time's operations Wordsworth explains how the unthinking 'vulgar joy' of the child resulted in 'chance collisions and quaint accidents' which somehow produced unforgettable images to be stored in the mind until more mature experience could make use of them and search out their deepest meanings (609–24). The places where he had experienced these moments of hardly understood joy remain as witnesses to the experience, so that it is incorporated into the growing poet's deepest loving being (625–40). It is no wonder that after two such sections Wordsworth can end the book in confident mood, the 'wavering balance' of his mind fixed, seeing the road plain before him. Without being aware of it, he is writing not a preparation for a masterpiece, but the masterpiece itself, the grandest of Romantic process poems.

Book II, 'School-time (Continued)', falls into two sections, the division coming between lines 180 and 181. The first takes up the distinction already established in the final section of the previous book between boisterous childhood and the beginnings of a subtler, calmer awareness of nature, and furnishes some specific examples of the way in which natural calm made itself felt in social activities – the recreations on Windermere, and the excursion to Furness Abbey with its 'more than inland peace / Left by the sea wind passing overhead' (115–16). Wordsworth encapsulates the combination of energy and peace in a line which is to be repeated later in the poem, describing part of the journey back from Furness: 'We beat with thundering hoofs the level sand' (144). It is this underlying calm that, as he explains in the opening lines of the book, unites himself as adult (writing in 1798-99) with the boy of twenty years before, who appears almost a different person because of his restless energy:

> A tranquillizing spirit presses now
> On my corporeal frame: so wide appears
> The vacancy between me and those days,
> Which yet have such self-presence in my mind
> That, sometimes, when I think of them, I seem
> Two consciousnesses, conscious of myself
> And of some other Being.
>
> (27–33)

This opening sets the subsequent incidents in context and reminds the reader again that the descriptions are the result of long brooding by the mature poet in the light of his more recent experience.

Wordsworth makes the transition to the rich and seminal second section by means of a short paragraph on the sun and the moon (181–202), distinguishing between his immediate intense mystical experience of them in boyhood and his more sober sacramental adult appreciation.[21] He announces the second section proper clearly:

> Those incidental charms which first attached
> My heart to rural objects, day by day
> Grew weaker, and I hasten on to tell
> How Nature, intervenient till this time,
> And secondary, now at length was sought
> For her own sake.
>
> (203–8)

For some years Nature is to be predominant, before it in turn leads Wordsworth to a deeper love of humanity. The statement of the theme is accompanied by an invocation of Coleridge (215–37) to emphasise that such attempts to analyse the development of feelings must be tentative and imperfect, so complex is the subject. By giving remembered incidents full sway Wordsworth allows imaginative richness to survive that abstract categorisation which Coleridge had rightly rejected:

> Thou art no slave
> Of that false secondary power, by which
> In weakness we create distinctions, then
> Deem that our puny boundaries are things
> Which we perceive, and not which we have made.
> To thee, unblinded by these outward shows,
> The unity of all has been revealed.
>
> (220–6)

The Coleridgean search for unity, for the imaginative unifying factor (such as the dancing in 'I wandered lonely as a Cloud') reinforced a crucial Wordsworthian cast of mind, which he traces back in this section to the rapport established between baby and mother, leading to a reciprocity between active mind and active universe. Of the babe he writes: 'From nature largely he receives; nor so / Is satisfied,

but largely gives again' (267–8). The chronology is somewhat unclear in the passage that follows, as 'a trouble came
into my mind / From unknown causes. I was left alone, /
Seeking the visible word, nor knowing why' (291–3). It
may be that Wordsworth is here obliquely describing the
effects of his mother's death when he was eight, reinforced
by his father's death five years later, and that those
psychological critics are right who maintain that he found,
without recognising the fact, in the natural world a
substitute for dead parents.[22] He introduces at this point a
concern which is to be prominent in the later part of the
poem: the sense that in intimate, visionary contact with the
natural world the child has accumulated a store of
experiences which, though not recollected precisely, can
nevertheless (indeed perhaps because of the imprecision) be a
constant inspiration to the adult, a goal to be striven for if
never attained, the impulse behind the process poem:

> . . . the soul,
> Remembering how she felt, but what she felt
> Remembering not, retains an obscure sense
> Of possible sublimity, to which,
> With growing faculties she doth aspire,
> With faculties still growing, feeling still
> That whatsoever point they gain, they still
> Have something to pursue.
>
> (334–41)

In this visionary experience Wordsworth recognises the pre-
eminent power of sound to 'breathe an elevated mood, by
form / Or image unprofaned' (325–6), where language
almost buckles under the strain of conveying the intensity of
the experience. He also insists, to pre-empt any charge of
vagueness or unreality, that the loving relationship between
boy and Nature results in a perception of minute details and
distinctions, 'difference / Perceived in things, where to the
common eye, / No difference is' (318–20). *The Prelude* is
often a very elevated poem, but Wordsworth mentions from
time to time the minuteness of observation reawakened in
him by his sister, which was to result in the superbly
perceptive, and practical, handbook *A Guide through the
District of the Lakes* (the final version appeared in 1835): here,

it helps to guarantee his experiences against the threat of insanity by wedding his feelings to the rocks and stones and trees of the phenomenal world. A further dominant theme in this rich section is the crucial role played by the human mind. At the age of seventeen, Wordsworth experienced a joy in the oneness of life, as he 'saw one life, and felt that it was joy' (430). Later in the poem the mind is to be recognised as pre-eminent, but at this point mind and Nature are mutually reinforcing as they had been for the babe, for, though the phraseology is consciously audacious and there are strong hints of what is to come, the active mind is for the most part subordinate to, disciplined by, the external world:

> But let this at least
> Be not forgotten, that I still retained
> My first creative sensibility,
> That by the regular action of the world
> My soul was unsubdued. A plastic power
> Abode with me, a forming hand, at times
> Rebellious, acting in a devious mood,
> A local spirit of its own, at war
> With general tendency, but for the most
> Subservient strictly to the external things
> With which it communed. An auxiliar light
> Came from my mind which on the setting sun
> Bestowed new splendor; the melodious birds,
> The gentle breezes, fountains that ran on,
> Murmuring so sweetly in themselves, obeyed
> A like dominion: and the midnight storm
> Grew darker in the presence of my eye.
> Hence my obeisance, my devotion hence,
> And hence my transport.

(377–95)

When Wordsworth adds to all of this the assertion, familiar from 'Tintern Abbey', that contact with the natural world produces an ennobling public moral effect (435–66), one may feel that he has almost earned his rather strained concluding claim of brotherhood with Coleridge in solitary worship of Nature and potential blessing to mankind.

Wordsworth's argument becomes somewhat less complex in Book III, 'Residence at Cambridge', which may again be seen as falling into two sections, the transition coming at lines 195–201. The main burden of the first section is the poet's increasing awareness of his own mind as, removed from the mountains though not altogether from the natural world, he habitually left his Cambridge companions.

>   perused
> The common countenance of earth and heaven;
> And, in turning the mind in upon itself,
> Pored, watched, expected, listened.
>
>   (110–13)

Thus when towards the end of the section Wordsworth addresses Coleridge, on a metaphorical eminence in his poetic journey, it is to assert the predominance of the mind's power (171–81). This looks forward unmistakably to the concluding lines of the whole poem, where the mind of man is 'A thousand times more beautiful than the earth / On which he dwells'.

In a sense this conclusion of the first section is also the end of a larger introductory movement of the poem. Wordsworth has established the grounds of his vision. He is descending from an eminence, now in his description of Cambridge and more completely as he moves on to London and France.[23] His cast of mind – visionary, solitary, unitary – has been settled and is to underlie his treatment of the haunts of men in England and abroad. Constantly under threat of corruption, dilution, or even destruction, his imaginative inner life is to waver, almost ceasing to be, till in the final books it is restored to something less intense and powerful but more sustained and knowing, under Dorothy's influence.

The more subdued second section of Book III, following the initial descent from the eminence, contrasts the super-ficiality of Cambridge undergraduate life with the various ways in which the imaginative vision persists – in response to the great Cantabrigians of the past (259–328), in a gradual approach to the world of men better suited to Wordsworth's 'visionary mind' than a sudden immersion would have been

(542–63), and in comparisons between dons, aged trees, and elderly shepherds at home (572–89); so that, while much at Cambridge was eminently forgettable, Wordsworth is able to conclude that 'something to the memory sticks at last, / Whence profit may be drawn in times to come' (667–8).

Book IV, 'Summer Vacation', may be envisaged as having four sections, each rising to a striking climax (1–180, 181–246, 247–345, 345–end). Its chief purpose is to reinforce Wordsworth's sense of purpose and perspective, as vacations ought to do.

The first section recounts the student's delighted rediscovery of the familiar pleasures of Hawkshead – friends, bed, dog – culminating in a walk round Esthwaite Water on a raw evening which inexplicably results in a vague but powerful sense of human potential, in the presence of God and of the natural world with its strange breath-like sounds. This is followed by a section on the change in Hawkshead folk and an appreciation of the admirable Ann Tyson, who was in effect Wordsworth's foster-mother, preparing the way naturally for the announcement of a fresh stage in his relationship with the natural world to which he brings a new tender human feeling (222–46). The boat image already quoted is an appropriate preparation for the third section, since its memorable embodiment of the complexity of self-scrutiny over a period of time leads into a recognition that even in this time of restoration and growing human-heartedness 'there was an inner falling-off' (270) resulting from the self-centred pursuit of 'vanities' and 'trivial pleasures' (288, 305). As a biblical text will take on animate form to accuse Bunyan in his autobiography *Grace Abounding*, so at the climax of this third section 'The memory of one particular hour / Doth here rise up against me' (315–16): it is the baptismal dedication of Wordsworth as a poet, the font being his own full heart, after a night of revelry, on a morning of uncommon splendour (balancing the raw evening at the end of the first section). To emphasise the importance of the crucial past moment Wordsworth turns to Coleridge in the present:

> Ah! need I say, dear Friend, that to the brim
> My heart was full? I made no vows, but vows
> Were then made for me; bond unknown to me
> Was given, that I should be, else sinning greatly,
> A dedicated Spirit. On I walked
> In blessedness, which even yet remains.
>
> (340–5)

The last section of this finely structured book selects one of the 'primitive hours' which, in spite of the general falling off, came to the young man, entirely without conscious preparation on his part and striking his exhausted and vacant mind with visionary force, the unforgettable meeting with the discharged soldier, an infinitely resonant spot of time embodying the mystery and bleak dignity of humanity. Most unusually and effectively, Wordsworth allows this to reverberate in the reader's mind as the book ends without further analysis.

The first of the two retrospective books, Book V, has an introduction (1–165), followed by a progression to an imaginative core at lines 389–481 and a set of supporting observations on the subject indicated by its title, 'Books'.[24]

The introduction consists of a solemn meditation developing the apocalyptic fear of final nakedness into a lamentation on the transience and fragility of those books in which humankind's achievement is notably enshrined:

> Oh! why hath not the mind
> Some element to stamp her image on
> In nature somewhat nearer to her own?
> Why, gifted with such powers to send abroad
> Her spirit, must it lodge in shrines so frail?
>
> (44–8)

The remarkable dream which illustrates this fear (attributed to a friend in 1805, but to the poet himself in 1850) is itself an example of the imaginative vision which certain rich books can inspire, for the dreamer has been reading Cervantes, and the Quixote-like Arab is partly out of the *Arabian Nights*. It involves the rider's crazy attempt to rescue geometry (scientific knowledge) and prophetic poetry

71

(imaginative knowledge with power) from a cataclysmic natural disaster. The passage may be felt to have already adequately compensated for the previous neglect of books by the time that Wordsworth apologises to Coleridge for that unpardonable omission (180–4). His main concern in the paragraphs (223–388) leading up to the climactic central portion of the book is to extol the virtues of unrestricted reading for children: his own mother had encouraged this, and had not sought to make him a precocious intellectual devoid of romance. He urges those who have charge of youthful minds to realise 'That in the unreasoning progress of the world / A wiser Spirit is at work for us' (384–5) than their restrictive prescriptions would allow.

Most appropriately, Wordsworth inserts here (389–422) the Boy of Winander fragment already published in the 1800 *Lyrical Ballads*. The story is intended to provide an example of the 'wiser Spirit' at work, and it is particularly fitting because it encapsulates the closeness of death to young life. At Hawkshead the graveyard 'hangs' immediately above the Elizabethan grammar school which Wordsworth attended, so here he places a richly complete short natural life cheek by jowl with a picture of real, vital children at the school (which should be set against any tendency to regard Wordsworth as an undiscriminating idealiser of childhood):

> A race of real children, not too wise,
> Too learned, or too good; but wanton, fresh,
> And bandied up and down by love and hate;
> Fierce, moody, patient, venturous, modest, shy;
> Mad at their sports like withered leaves in winds;
> Though doing wrong, and suffering, and full oft
> Bending beneath our life's mysterious weight
> Of pain and fear; yet still in happiness
> Not yielding to the happiest upon earth.
>
> (436–44)

For these children, free reading and natural vision will result in 'Knowledge not purchased with the loss of power' (449), resembling that combination of truth and beauty which Keats was to seek, abstract knowledge and its concrete and effective moving embodiment in words.

While the reader is still on this high imaginative level

Wordsworth chooses to introduce the incident of the drowned man, a narration so powerful as to be in danger of obscuring the point that it is there made to illustrate:

> The succeeding day,
> (Those unclaimed garments telling a plain Tale)
> Went there a Company, and, in their Boat
> Sounded with grappling irons, and long poles.
> At length, the dead Man, 'mid that beauteous scene
> Of trees, and hills and water, bolt upright
> Rose with his ghastly face; a spectre shape
> Of terror even! and yet no vulgar fear,
> Young as I was, a Child not nine years old,
> Possessed me, for my inner eye had seen
> Such sights before, among the shining streams
> Of Fairy Land, the Forests of Romance:
> Thence came a spirit hallowing what I saw
> With decoration and ideal grace;
> A dignity, a smoothness, like the works
> Of Grecian Art, and purest Poesy.
>
> (466–81)

The belief that romantic reading can inoculate a child against common fear in the face of such an incident may be questioned, but this is the poet's interpretation in 1804 of his experience and may be more widely valid than might at first appear.

After this double imaginative climax of Boy of Winander and drowned man, the remainder of the book explores in more detail the child's experience of books, the *Arabian Nights* taking pride of place (482–500), along with the creations of all 'dreamers' and 'Forgers of lawless tales' (547–8), and it notes a fresh stage in Wordsworth's development not recorded in the earlier books, the love of words which developed around the age of thirteen (575–81). The discussion gives Wordsworth an opportunity in conclusion to echo the drowned man episode by paying tribute to the strange power of words to transfigure and glorify the poet's subject matter (619–29).

Book VI, as its title, 'Cambridge and the Alps', indicates, falls into two distinct sections joined by a substantial transitional passage at lines 208–331. The resumed description of Cambridge introduces in turn: a further advocacy of free study (19–54); Wordsworth's growing literary self-confidence with high hopes which he still now retains in 1804 at the age of thirty-four (55–79); a spot of time with a tranquil vision beneath an ash tree (80–109); a rather obscure assertion that Nature guided him in his reading by directing his thoughts, by which he may mean that a sense of grandeur and proportion was vital in his experience of literature (110–34); and his study of geometry, which had for him a spiritual purity as embodying the laws which govern the natural universe (135–87). For all the positive contributions which Cambridge made, Wordsworth leaves it on a negative note with a description of youthful melancholy, idleness, and lack of intensity (188–207) and turns with relief to the transitional address to Dorothy his sister, Mary his childhood companion and at the time of writing his wife of two years, and especially Coleridge. It is appropriate that as he sets about his account of his first European journey, the beginning of a process lasting several years which was to end in mental breakdown, he should allude to the sustaining feminine companionship which preceded and succeeded that period and to Coleridge's journey to the Mediterranean in a search for health (as it turned out, a vain one). It is poignant, too, that on the edge of recalling an ultimately deeply distressing period in his life, Wordsworth should lament that he did not meet Coleridge until long after their student days at Cambridge, observing that had he known him then, he might, with his own calm and steadiness of mind derived from Nature, have 'chased away the airy wretchedness / That battened on thy youth' (325–6).

The second section of this sixth book, describing the humble version of the Grand Tour undertaken by Wordsworth and his friend Robert Jones, falls into three parts. There is a straightforward account of the excitement of early revolutionary France (332–487), greatly deepened by the addition in the 1850 version of the passage regretting the destruction of the Grande Charteuse monastery alluded to above. The central section describing the crossing of the Alps (488–580), disappointing at the time, momentously significant in retrospect with the full confrontation of the

Imagination in 1804, is analysed in detail in the final part of this chapter. After the mighty apocalyptic *pathos* Wordsworth relaxes in the paradisal *ethos* of Lake Como (581–616), but uneasy reverberations persist in the account of the disorientation caused by unfamiliar clocks (617–57). The book concludes with an attempt to sum up in two of the dominant images of the poem, stream and wind, the effect of these experiences of the mind, emphasising once more the dual poles of *pathos* and *ethos*, grandeur and tenderness:

> Finally, whate'er
> I saw, or heard, or felt, was but a stream
> That flowed into a kindred stream, a gale
> That helped me forwards, did administer
> To grandeur and to tenderness, to the one
> Directly, but to tender thoughts by means
> Less often instantaneous in effect.
>
> (672–8)

Book VII, 'Residence in London', is structured around an opposition between superficiality and profundity, the surface and the depths. Its movement is somewhat less clearly defined than those of earlier books, but it may be regarded as having two principal sections (the division coming after line 516), each consisting of a superficial view of the city deepening into visionary significance. The book begins (and ends) with reference to the natural world. Its introductory paragraph describes how Wordsworth has been able to resume the poem after a gap of several months in the summer of 1804: the autumn breezes again indicate inspiration. The fitness of this opening lies not purely in its obvious contrast with the subject of the book which it helps to frame, but in its preparation for the way in which Wordsworth constantly sees and judges London in the light of his rural experiences. So in the first section proper, after he has described his move to the city (57–80) and his early childhood idealisation of the place (81–138), he uses natural parallels to suggest the soothing effect of quiet nooks in the bustling metropolis (139–204):

> Meanwhile the roar continues, till at length,

Escaped as from an enemy, we turn
Abruptly into some sequestered nook
Still as a sheltered place when winds blow loud.

(184–7)

There follows a series of observations stressing the randomness of London (205–32), its diversity (233–43), and the liveliness of its entertainments (244–310). Then comes the section's climax with a sudden deepening, much more sustained than the brief repose in the quiet nooks. Wordsworth has seen a strange version of the story of the Maid of Buttermere, the daughter of a Cumbrian innkeeper who had been betrayed into a bigamous marriage. She functions in the London scene as a radical innocent, reminding Wordsworth of 'those ingenuous moments of our youth, / Ere yet by use we have learned to slight the crimes / And sorrows of the world' (362–4). The experiences of seeing her story told in a London theatre and of writing these 'memorial verses' prepare the way for two imaginatively conceived figures. First there is the beautiful boy on his mother's knee amid a dissolute theatrical mob, seeming 'A sort of alien scattered from the clouds' (378), who would most fittingly be spared exposure to the world of Experience like the Maid of Buttermere's dead infant (399–412). The other figure, in total contrast, is the first woman whom Wordsworth heard blaspheming, encountered on his initial journey to Cambridge but inserted here for the shocking contrast. (Given the urban subject matter one might detect a parallel to the structural use of contrasting characters by Pope, notably in the *Moral Essays*.)

Wordsworth is to prolong this section a little by a meditation on the state of his imagination during his London stay (489–516), but this meditation is preceded by a pleasant but at first rather inconsequential general picture of the brightness of theatres – superficial indeed, yet with something of deeper import caught from childhood excitement at rude rural shows and summed up in the extraordinary final parallel (too extraordinary for retention in 1850):

Enchanting age and sweet!
Romantic almost, looked at through a space,
How small of intervening years! For then,

76

Though surely no mean progress had been made
In meditations holy and sublime,
Yet something of a girlish child-like gloss
Of novelty survived for scenes like these;
Pleasure that had been handed down from times
When, at a Country-Playhouse, having caught,
In summer, through the fractured wall, a glimpse
Of daylight, at the thought of where I was
I gladdened more than if I had beheld
Before me some bright cavern of Romance,
Or than we do, when on our beds we lie
At night, in warmth, when rains are beating hard.

(474–88)

The meditation which follows is the key to the whole book. It begins with a rather ingenuous defence of material which to many will seem 'neither dignified enough / Nor arduous', included because it forms part of the building up of his own mind, and therefore 'not to be despised / By those who have observed the curious props / By which the perishable hours of life / Rest on each other, and the world of thought / Exists and is sustained' (489–95). Yet Wordsworth acknowledges that generally in London, as in Cambridge, imagination slept even during a period when the heart was being moved by human sufferings. Only occasionally could the faculty find material adequate to its own powers:

                           . . . all this
       Passed not beyond the suburbs of the mind:
       If aught there were of real grandeur here
       'Twas only then when gross realities,
       The incarnation of the Spirits that moved
       Amid the Poet's beauteous world, called forth,
       With that distinctness which a contrast gives
       Or opposition, made me recognize
       As by a glimpse, the things which I had shaped
       And yet not shaped, had seen, and scarcely seen,
       Had felt, and thought of in my solitude.

(506–16)

There were then in London certain moments which seemed to crystallise with a peculiar intensity matters which had been only dimly apprehended in Wordsworth's earlier life. Two of these moments – the Maid of Buttermere and the blaspheming woman (credited to London) – have been noted as part of this first culmination; another will furnish the climax of the book's second section.

This second section (beginning at line 517) is, after the depth of the Buttermere episode and the central meditation, openly satirical, attacking the superficiality of fashionable secular and religious rhetorics and manners (517–87). The deepening which follows is more profound than the corresponding moment in the first section, and it is again signalled by an address to Coleridge (593–8). In moments of vision the crowds pass by like ghostly processions, or as in a dream, so that Wordsworth experiences a sense of total unfamiliarity and disorientation as that mystery of human life which the city so often effectively disguises, and of which we understand so little, rises to the surface with disturbing and elevating power:

> . . . the shapes before my eyes became
> A second-sight procession, such as glides
> Over still mountains, or appears in dreams;
> And all the ballast of familiar life,
> The present, and the past; hope, fear; all stays,
> All laws of acting, thinking, speaking man
> Went from me, neither knowing me, nor known.
> And once, far-travelled in such mood, beyond
> The reach of common indications, lost
> Amid the moving pageant, 'twas my chance
> Abruptly to be smitten with the view
> Of a blind Beggar, who, with upright face,
> Stood propped against a Wall, upon his Chest
> Wearing a written paper, to explain
> The story of the Man, and who he was.
> My mind did at this spectacle turn round
> As with the might of waters, and it seemed
> To me that in this Label was a type,
> Or emblem, of the utmost that we know;
> Both of ourselves and of the universe;
> And, on the shape of the unmoving man,

His fixèd face and sightless eyes, I looked
As if admonished from another world.

(601–23)

Wordsworth is aware of the inability of words to tell more
than a limited amount about the world and its inhabitants,
but such an imaginative use of language as this passage
exhibits can at least arouse awareness of what cannot be
said, so that the reader's own mind too may 'turn
round / As with the might of waters' as Wordsworth's did
before the beggar and the leech-gatherer.

In the final lines of the book Wordsworth remains on this
high imaginative level, distinguishing between scenes where
the mind can be active and those, typified by Bartholomew
Fair, where it is overwhelmed, resulting in 'blank confusion'
(696) and needing the steady perception of underlying form
learnt among the mountains to produce from the chaos of
'self-destroying, transitory things' his ultimate goal, 'Composure and ennobling harmony' (740–1).[25]

Book VIII, the second retrospective book, 'Love of Nature
Leading to Love of Mankind', has been much disparaged.
Jonathan Wordsworth goes so far as to remark: 'It is
unusually plain that Wordsworth has nothing to say.'[26]
Even for those who can follow Wordsworth into his
metaphysical and apocalyptic speculations there are likely to
be moments in this long book when the eyes feel heavy.
There are two principal problems. In the first place,
Wordsworth is recapitulating, not as in Book V to fill in a
subject which he had entirely neglected in his account
thitherto, but to bring out and emphasise that growing
awareness of humanity which most readers will already have
perceived in the poem as it has developed. The danger is
that he will merely repeat himself. A second problem is that
he cites very few specific examples, so that the book is
almost entirely theoretical, and though Wordsworth's
theorising is usually of great interest and often poetically of
high quality, nearly nine hundred lines of it, with few
alleviations, is a good deal too much.

The book consists of a long first section, with several
subdivisions, covering again the country period (to line

640), followed by much shorter sections on Cambridge (641–77) and London (678–end).

The opening description of the fair at the base of Helvellyn is structurally helpful. It acts as a contrasting link with the bewilderingly complex Bartholomew Fair which ended the previous book, since the rural event attracts 'but a little Family of Men' (7) and presents humanity and Nature in intimate harmony:

> For all things serve them; them the Morning light
> Loves as it glistens on the silent rocks,
> And them the silent Rocks, which now from high
> Look down upon them; the reposing Clouds,
> The lurking Brooks from their invisible haunts,
> And Old Helvellyn, conscious of the stir,
> And the blue Sky that roofs their calm abode.
>
> (55–61)

The main burden of this first long section is that, just as the Lake District is more truly impressive than fabled paradises (119–43), so those common shepherd folk whom Wordsworth has been led by Nature to appreciate are superior to their idealised counterparts in classical pastoral. He is thus again justifying his choice of the everyday in order to bring out something of a grandeur and mystery most clearly seen in the context of the natural environment. So it was particular conjunctions of shepherd and natural phenomena which drew his affections beyond the family circle (62–119) and led him to understand that such wider affections had, unlike the products of idealised pastoral, beneficial moral consequences both for the individual and for his life in society,

> Conducted on to individual ends
> Or social, and still followed by a train
> Unwooed, unthought-of even, simplicity,
> And beauty, and inevitable grace.
>
> (155–8)

Wordsworth stresses that this is an unconscious process in which Nature and ordinary common humanity fasten 'on the heart / Insensibly' (159–72). What excited him most was not recollections of charming old pastoral customs but local tales of suffering (173–221), of which he presents as the only extended example in the book the story of the lost sheep (222–311). This is a plain tale indeed, but it is well told with several fine imaginative touches. (It must have struck the older Wordsworth as too unremarkable, and 1850 eliminates it with deleterious effect on the whole book.) It was possibly intended to form the apex of this rural first section, but for some readers the subsequent extended meditation (353–471) will be more intense with its passing by of German pastoral, as observed during the Goslar period (312–53), in favour of the northern shepherd's life – described in terms recalling 'Michael' (353–428) – which introduces the poet's heart 'To an unconscious love and reverence / Of human nature' (413–14) and acts as a protection against meanness of spirit (428–71). In a careful cautionary note, Wordsworth makes it clear that long after the period here recapitulated, indeed until his second trip to France at the age of twenty-two or twenty-three, humanity was still subordinate to Nature in his affections (472–97). After a rather inconsequential general paragraph on the different occupations of country folk (498–510), well omitted in 1850, he deals with a short phase in his view of rural humankind during which, as a potential artist, he had tended to embroider incidents fancifully, though since (unlike Coleridge) he was always in touch with 'a real solid world / Of images' (604–5) it did no real harm (511–623). This transient phase was followed by 'a time of greater dignity' when he came to experience the 'pulse of being' or one life permeating man and Nature (624–40).

The brief section on Cambridge (641–77), unmemorable in its phrasing, presents a strangely dark picture as Wordsworth thinks of human 'guilt and wretchedness . . . / With an indefinite terror and dismay' but with a growing moral awareness and a faith that has remained with him 'that by acting well / And understanding, I should learn to love / The end of life and every thing we know'.

The concluding section on London provides an opportunity to handle the city in a more ideal manner, stressing the power and unity of the metropolis, the grandeur rather than the pettiness, relieved by scenes of tenderness such as the father and baby (836–59): 1850 transfers this to the

previous book, where its specificity is needed less. Wordsworth ends the book with yet another progress report:
Nature is still predominant, but Man is ascending in the
poet's consciousness.

Book IX, 'Residence in France', presents few problems to
the reader, except on occasion the difficulty of sustaining
interest in such an exceedingly unadorned narrative. The
opening echo of Book IX of *Paradise Lost*, where Milton
turns to tragic matter, is witty and decorative rather than
deeply functional, but there are suggestions of a personal
paradise being lost. The chief point to note is Wordsworth's
belief that his natural republicanism had its origin in his
democratic schooling, which makes his allusions to Latin
political writings here and in the following book peculiarly
fitting.[27] Wordsworth's return to France in 1791 was
primarily intended to help him 'speak the language more
familiarly' (37) with a tutor's profession in mind, but the
republican cause and his relationship with Annette Vallon
involved him more deeply than he had anticipated with that
nation. The narrative reaches a memorable climax in
Beaupuy's agitated indication of the peasant girl as a specific
example of what he and his companions are fighting against
(511–34). In 1850 Wordsworth recognised this as a height
not to be stooped from (1850: 541) and provided a summary
of the Vaudracour and Julia tale which is actually much
more effective as a strong ending to the book than the full
version included in 1805: self-censorship can on occasion be
aesthetically beneficial.

Book X, 'Residence in France and French Revolution',
continues the plain narrative to cover Wordsworth's return
to England, his isolation and breakdown, and the announcement of his recovery under Dorothy's care. Again one may
observe how his confidence in the ordinary man underlies
his analysis of political extremism in revolutionary France
and reactionary Britain (83–128, 567–656). It is this which
makes his sense of isolation so poignant when he is unable
to join in prayer with those whom he has been taught to
love and esteem:

The Prelude (1805)

> It was a grief,
> Grief call it not, 'twas anything but that,
> A conflict of sensations without name,
> Of which he only who may love the sight
> Of a Village Steeple as I do can judge,
> When in the Congregation, bending all
> To their great Father, prayers were offered up
> Or praises for our Country's Victories,
> And 'mid the simple worshippers, perchance,
> I only, like an uninvited Guest
> Whom no one owned sate silent, shall I add,
> Fed on the day of vengeance yet to come!
>
> (263–74)

In the turbulence of Wordsworth's feelings at this crisis there are agony and nightmare at news of the Terror in France (307–80), a Nature-inspired prophetic awareness of the reservoir of guilt which has led to the present period of excess (381–439), memories alternately refreshing and tormenting of the first happy days in France (440–65) and, concluding the first half of the book with good effect at the point where 1850 divides it into two, the news of Robespierre's death (466–566).[28] It should be noted that when he hears the news, Wordsworth has just visited the grave at Cartmel of William Taylor, the teacher who had taught him to love poetry and who had died in his early thirties. A major theme at this stage of the poem is Wordsworth's alienation not only from his fellows but from the past, personal and historical. Robespierre represents such a public discontinuity, the poet's visit to Taylor's grave a personal continuity. It is a structural masterstroke to repeat, after the announcement of Robespierre's death and his own utterance of thanksgiving, phrases from the passage in Book II describing the boys' excursion to Furness Abbey 'In wantonness of heart', for such an unalloyed joy had hardly been experienced since boyhood (559–66; cf. II, 99–144).

The second section of Book X (Book XI in 1850) is a little confusing at the outset, for after the passage already alluded to where Wordsworth declares his continued trust in the people and rejects alarmist British reactionary rumours about France (567–656), he doubles back without warning to

83

recapitulate his Nature-inspired hopes for the Revolution while in France (657–735). But this is so that he may the more powerfully describe how the crisis associated with the Terror and the declaration of war by Britain in 1794 led him to adopt the specious optimistic benevolism of William Godwin, and in due course, disillusioned with this and seeking absolute certainty, to yield up moral questions in despair and turn to mathematics (757–904).

The process of restoration initiated by Dorothy and Coleridge is to be the subject of Books XI and XII. For the moment Wordsworth merely states the bare fact in an address to Coleridge (904–40) and ends with a wish that his friend may be restored to health in a sadly degenerate Sicily, which yet reminds him of that continuity between past and present whose recovery in his own life he is about to celebrate:

> There is
> One great Society alone on earth
> The noble Living and the noble Dead.

(967–9)

Book XI, 'Imagination, How Impaired and Restored', consists of a single cumulative movement, striking the reader powerfully after the less imaginatively cohesive and exalted form of the previous three books. Wordsworth characteristically begins with a slight backtracking from the point of recovery and spends the first part of the book (1–199) describing from a different point of view his years of alienation. Now he stresses that Nature was never wholly absent, but that he had scented her fragrances from afar like a mariner forbidden to land:

> My business was upon the barren seas,
> My errand was to sail to other coasts.

(55–6)

Cut off from the past on Godwinian principles, aggressively rationalistic, he had adopted a superficial attitude even to Nature, the eye becoming dominant, the heart failing, as in the first visit to the Wye described in 'Tintern Abbey' (XI, 57–199). From all such perversions Dorothy had remained

84

free (199–223), and under her influence he recovered that first imaginative sensibility:

> I had felt
> Too forcibly, too early in my life,
> Visitings of imaginative power
> For this to last: I shook the habit off
> Entirely and for ever, and again
> In Nature's presence stood, as I stand now,
> A sensitive, and a creative soul.
>
> (251–7)

The two momentous 'spots of time' which demonstrate the fusing of present creation and past childhood experience – the gibbet episode and his father's death – make a memorable double climax to the book: they are both sources of bleak visionary power from which the adult poet can 'drink, / As at a fountain' (384–5).

Book XII, continuing the same subject, has a similarly unified climactic structure, but with a curious twist at the end. Wordsworth explores the way in which Nature's main gift, a sense of proportion, has led him to write about the humblest people and objects, imitating her consecration of them. This is a lucid and passionate argument, which will repay the closest scrutiny. However, just as one is prepared for a specimen of such a consecrating poetry, Wordsworth introduces a fresh argument with the habitual signposting provided by a supportive invocation of Coleridge:

> Dearest Friend,
> Forgive me if I say that I, who long
> Had harboured reverentially a thought
> That Poets, even as Prophets, each with each
> Connected in a mightly scheme of truth,
> Have each for his peculiar dower, a sense
> By which he is enabled to perceive
> Something unseen before; forgive me, Friend,
> If I, the meanest of this Band, had hope
> That unto me had also been vouchsafed
> An influx, that in some sort I possessed
> A privilege, and that a work of mine,

Proceeding from the depth of untaught things,
Enduring and creative, might become
A power like one of Nature's.

(298–312)

One is now in the presence of something less clear and lucid
– a poetry 'proceeding from the depth of untaught things'
resulting in something as powerful, definitive, and inexplicable as Nature herself, and the supporting example is taken
from one of the weirdest of Wordsworth's experiences, that
solitary walk across Salisbury Plain in 1793 which had
already resulted in the haunting early poem 'Salisbury Plain'
(Gill, pp. 13–28). The irruption into the poem of this reverie
with its amoral linking of living and dead is most
extraordinary. Wordsworth's transition back to the central
theme of the book, 'This for the past . . .' (354), is
inadequate (probably intentionally so), and the reader is left
stunned by a *pathos* which cannot be wholly tempered or
tamed to the consecrating service of humankind.

The final book consists of a vision, a meditation, and an
extended coda. The opening is masterly: the title 'Conclusion'
followed by an unannounced account of the (typically
unexpected) Snowdon vision and a profound analysis which
moves in the direction of Wordsworth's later poetry with its
overtly symbolic handling of Nature, but as yet without any
loss of power, so that the effect is one of majestic firmness.
The coda, beginning at line 211, with its series of personal
addresses and tributes, is structurally perfect after the
preceding heights, a reversal of the usual climactic structure
so as to end in ever-increasing calm. In order, Wordsworth
takes up: Dorothy's gentleness modifying his natural
sternness (211–46); Coleridge's unitary thought and his
humanity (246–68); the omissions in the poem, notably of
Fancy and variety of character (269–331); Raisley Calvert's
legacy which had enabled him to pursue his vocation
(332–67); and finally Coleridge's hope for a great work from
his friend's pen (367–end). Whatever difficulties the poem
may have presented to its readers, however great the
demands it has made, its conclusion is suffused with a
radiant and benign clarity.

Several of the techniques necessary for a responsive reading of *The Prelude* can be conventionally illustrated by a close examination of the passage in Book VI describing the crossing of the Alps. This consists of four paragraphs (488–524, 525–48, 549–72, and 573–80). Each is different in manner, contributing to a complex presentation of those three hours which were at the time extraordinarily impressive and which acquired more and more meaning with the passage of the years.[29]

The first paragraph is basically a narrative of the events leading up to the crossing, but it is prefaced by lines (488–94) linking it with the events which have just been recorded. In the preceding paragraphs Wordsworth has been describing his first encounter with the Alps. Mont Blanc failed to live up to expectations, to satisfy his imaginative conception of what it ought to be, and consequently his 'under-thirst / of vigour' is unsatisfied by what have essentially been typical tourist's 'delights', mingled with an affected 'Dejection taken up for pleasure's sake' (482). The event which he is about to describe will involve a 'Far different dejection', 'A deep and genuine sadness'. The first point to be made about this passage, as about *The Prelude* in general, is that one should beware of accepting Wordsworth's summary of what he is about to do or has done as a uniquely authoritative interpretation of the episode. Here there will indeed be dejection and sadness, but there is much else involved in the passage, and they are far from being its dominant theme.

The introductory lines conclude with a comment which may at first appear superfluous:

> The circumstances I will here relate
> Even as they were.

This is omitted in 1850, which has less regard for matter-of-factness than 1805. In the early version the sentence (or what it recalls to the reader's memory) is of crucial importance. Students of literature are nowadays brought up, quite rightly, to understand that when the personal pronoun 'I' occurs in a poem it is the narrator and not the poet who is designated. In *The Prelude*, however, as to a large extent in most of Wordsworth's poems apart from the dramatic lyrical ballads, 'I' is the poet, or at the very least a version of the poet. Wordsworth writes, in David Perkins's phrase, 'the poetry of sincerity'. Truth to his own experience, as he sees it, is vital in this poem. That does not mean, of course, that it is a literal account throughout. Long meditation on past events has brought out what Wordsworth sees as essential underlying truths, and often he combines incidents and alters their order with the intention of arriving at the deeper truth of poetry rather than that of history. But fidelity to his experience is crucial to him, earthing his imagination in particular experiences.

Two points of central importance for reading *The Prelude* are suggested by the remainder of this initial paragraph. The first, concerning the nature of the blank verse, is well made in general terms by Christopher Ricks in his essay 'William Wordsworth 1: "A Pure Organic Pleasure from the Lines"'.[30] He shows how Wordsworth artfully and subtly uses the divisions between the lines of his verse to reinforce his sense, not ostentatiously but gently and persistently. This is indeed an essential difference between run-of-the-mill blank verse and the verse of the great masters – Milton, Wordsworth himself, and supremely Shakespeare. Good blank verse is not simply chopped up prose. The point is well exemplified by this narrative:

> . . . we together ate
> Our noon's repast, from which the Travellers rose,
> Leaving us at the Board. Ere long we followed,
> Descending by the beaten road that led
> Right to a rivulet's edge, and there broke off.
> The only track now visible was one
> Upon the further side, right opposite,
> And up a lofty Mountain. This we took
> After a little scruple, and short pause,
> And climed with eagerness, though not, at length,
> Without surprise and some anxiety
> On finding that we did not overtake
> Our Comrades gone before.
>
> (499–511)

The 'rose' at the end of line 500, followed by the comma, slightly reinforces the sense in reading. So does the 'led' with the enjambement two lines later, followed by the 'broke off' at the end of the sentence and line. With Wordsworth, the reader looks across the rivulet to the track, 'one / Upon the further side', and sees it 'right opposite', at the end of the line. It is taken after a 'short pause' which the line ending with its comma invites the reader to share, and the final three lines imitate the anxiety of the travellers. In reading, of course, one is not consciously aware of any of this, but such quiet reinforcings of the sense are second nature to this poet and should become so to the sensitive reader.[31]

The other point suggested by this narrative should also be axiomatic for the reader who has advanced thus far in the poem. Wordsworth's matter-of-fact narratives are always metaphorical: he writes a species of continuous metaphor.[32] In 1805 he needed only to drop slight hints which the close circle addressed in the poem would understand. The travellers 'climbed with eagerness' (508) until they learned from the peasant that they 'must descend' (515) and that 'thenceforward all our course / Was downwards, with the current of that Stream' (518–19). The hapless peasant being re-questioned,

> all the answers which the Man returned
> To our inquiries, in their sense and substance,
> Translated by the feelings which we had,
> Ended in this; that we had crossed the Alps.
>
> (521–4)

In 1805 Wordsworth did not need to specify what the 'feelings' were, leaving his readers (or hearers) to gather them from the apparently plain narrative. 1850, revised for public consumption, makes everything very clear. The track 'held forth / Conspicuous invitation to ascend / A lofty mountain' (1850: 571–2), in tune with the travellers' expectations of a supreme experience awaiting them. The peasant explains that the correct path will be 'all plain to sight' (1850: 584), and in their disappointment the travellers are 'Loth to believe what we so grieved to hear, / For still we had hopes that pointed to the clouds' (1850: 568–7). Such explicit comments during the course of the narrative mean that the texture of the 1805 poem is less varied than 1850, the narrative approaching closer to the analytical sections. For the experienced reader they should not usually be necessary, though 1850 can on occasion help to clarify obscurities in the earlier version.

The second paragraph (525–48) is on first reading totally unexpected, and it never loses its power to astonish and thrill, even after many years' acquaintance. It is the most striking of all the occasions when the very time of writing is introduced into the poem. While Wordsworth is actually recounting this story of disappointed aspirations the Imagination does its work and makes clear the deep significance of the incident, the lesson which it holds for him and for humanity. Under the strain and excitement of the moment syntax buckles in 1805:

> Imagination! lifting up itself
> Before the eye and progress of my Song
> Like an unfathered vapour; here that Power,
> In all the might of its endowments, came
> Athwart me; I was lost as in a cloud,
> Halted, without a struggle to break through.
> And now recovering, to my Soul I say
> 'I recognise thy glory'.

(525–32)

Just how daringly expression mirrors process here is made clear by 1850's more logical, less striking version:

> Imagination – here the Power so called
> Through sad incompetence of human speech,
> That awful Power rose from the mind's abyss
> Like an unfathered vapour that enwraps,
> At once, some lonely traveller. I was lost;
> Halted without an effort to break through;
> But to my conscious soul I now can say –
> 'I recognise thy glory'.

(1850: 592–9)

That is by no means disastrous: the parallels between the writing of the episode and the alpine journey are made more heavily, so that it can plausibly be read as transferring the compositional experience back to the actual moments after the crossing, but the 'mind's abyss' is telling.[33] However, the vital spontaneity of 1805 is lost. In the earlier version the first three lines sound like an amazed acknowledgement of the power: only at the end of the third line does the poet decide how to proceed, and then he uses an excessive 'struggle' where 1850 more reasonably substitutes 'effort', and an illogical but typically powerful 'And' where 1850 has 'But'.[34] (The 'And' anticipates line 572, just as the 'Athwart' does the 'thwarting' in 560.) 1850 continues to be just that crucial bit less daring as normal 'sense' ceases to operate ('sense' is richly ambiguous here: common bodily experience, common sense, perhaps). Where 1805 reads:

> In such strength
> Of usurpation, in such visitings
> Of awful promise, when the light of sense
> Goes out in flashes that have shewn to us
> The invisible world, doth Greatness make abode,
>
> (532–6)

1850 has:

> in such strength
> Of usurpation, when the light of sense
> Goes out, but with a flash that has revealed
> The invisible world, doth greatness make abode.
>
> (1850: 599–602)

That second logical 'but' in 1850 makes the process a little clearer than it ought to be, and the loss of the boldly suggestive 'visitings / Of awful promise' is regrettable.

Lines 538 to the end of the paragraph are a classic expression of Romantic aspiration, at the heart of this supreme process poem. The aspiration may be vague, but the expression will repay the closest attention. The phrase 'blest in thoughts / That are their own perfection and reward' (555–6) may be seen as hinting at a whole aesthetics and morality of process thought. 1850 is mostly close to the original here, but the reader may care to read the endings of the two versions of the paragraph aloud to judge if the extension of the concluding simile strengthens or weakens the climax of the argument. The last two lines of 1805 read:

> Strong in itself, and in the access of joy
> Which hides it like the overflowing Nile.

These are replaced by four lines in 1850:

> Strong in herself and in beatitude
> That hides her, like the mighty flood of Nile
> Poured from his fount of Abyssinian clouds
> To fertilise the whole Egyptian plain.[35]

The third paragraph, almost entirely unchanged in 1850, suggests three points of the widest application. The view of the pass here presented combines more intimately than any other passage in Wordsworth extreme agitation and extreme underlying peace, in the form of a natural paradox:

> The immeasurable height
> Of woods decaying, never to be decayed,
> The stationary blasts of water-falls.
>
> (556–8)

Secondly, this agitation is suggested partly by a characteristic combination of dead metaphor and original energy in the 'Winds thwarting winds, bewildered and forlorn', literally crossing as well as thwarting in the modern abstract sense. John F. McCarthy suggests that dead metaphor 'gives Wordsworth a superpersonal sanction for his "animism" which is built into the language, a substitute for the repudiated mythological tradition'.[36] The final point concerns a parallel tonal ambiguity in the paragraph as pronounced as that in the second stanza of 'A slumber did my spirit seal'. Wordsworth has promised his readers an account of a dejection, but at the beginning of this paragraph he announces that 'The dull and heavy slackening that ensued / Upon those tidings by the Peasant given / Was soon dislodged'. After the intervening compositional ecstacy one might expect an unambiguous triumphant apocalypticism. The paragraph is certainly apocalyptic, beyond almost anything else in Wordsworth, but whether it is more comforting or disquieting it is difficult to say. The pass is 'gloomy', and the details of the natural scene are often frightening: of the extraordinary series of similes which ends the paragraph only the 'blossoms upon one tree' is necessarily pleasant to contemplate.

The brief concluding paragraph is the sort of detail which it is easy to overlook in reading such a long poem, and it is similarly ambiguous:

> That night our lodging was an Alpine House,
> An Inn, or Hospital, as they are named,
> Standing in that same valley by itself,
> And close upon the confluence of two Streams;
> A dreary Mansion, large beyond all need,
> With high and spacious rooms, deafened and stunned
> By noise of waters, making innocent Sleep
> Lie melancholy among weary bones.

With its picture of utter exhaustion this may be read as a confirmation of a deeply troubled reading of the experience to counterbalance the compositional ecstasy, or it may be the equivalent of Lily Briscoe's weary but triumphant feelings at the end of Virginia Woolf's *To the Lighthouse*:

Quickly, as if she were recalled by something over there, she turned to her canvas. There it was – her picture. Yes, with all its green and blues, its lines running up and across, its attempt at something. It would be hung in the attics, she thought, it would be destroyed. But what did that matter? she asked herself, taking up her brush again. She looked at the steps; they were empty; she looked at her canvas; it was blurred. With a sudden intensity, as if she saw it clear for a second, she drew a line there, in the centre. It was done; it was finished. Yes, she thought, laying down her brush in extreme fatigue, I have had my vision.[37]

CHAPTER 4

Poems, in Two Volumes
(1807)

In 1807 Wordsworth published a substantial but necessarily somewhat miscellaneous collection in two volumes of the shorter poems composed since January 1801. From this diversity a number of types, each representing a distinct development in his art, have been selected for examination here: what he was later to class as 'Poems of the Fancy'; poems of domestic affection; 'Moods of My Own Mind'; poems with Scottish subjects; sonnets; and the set of three great stoical pieces 'Resolution and Independence', 'Peele Castle' ('Elegiac Stanzas'), and the Immortality Ode.

'Poems of the Fancy': two daisy poems ('In youth from rock to rock I went' and 'With little here to do or see')

During Wordsworth's early years at Dove Cottage, he was much taken up with a study of the Elizabethan and seventeenth-century poets whose works were conveniently extracted in Robert Anderson's *Poets of Great Britain*, published in 1795. Ben Jonson, Michael Drayton, and George Wither were among those who particularly appealed to him at this period, and in 1815 he acknowledged the debt to Wither by prefixing to his poem 'To the Daisy' ('In youth from rock to rock') some lines (slightly altered) from *The Shepherd's Hunting. Eclogue 4*, which begins with a reference to Wither's muse:

Her divine skill taught me this,
That from every thing I saw
I could some instruction draw,
And raise pleasure to the height
Through the meanest object's sight.
By the murmur of a spring,
Or the least bough's rustelling;
By a Daisy whose leaves spread
Shut when Titan goes to bed;
Or a shady bush or tree;
She could more infuse in me
Than all Nature's beauties can
In some other wiser man.

Two of the 1807 daisy poems ('In youth from rock to rock' and 'With little here to do or see') are fine examples of a group of a dozen or so poems which take small subjects and consciously exercise the fancy upon them, moralising gently. There is humour and playfulness in the process, but the predominance of the fancy does not exclude imaginative seriousness. For Wordsworth, unlike Coleridge, the fancy was in her own way creative, and the distinction which he was to make in the 1815 *Poems* between 'Poems of the Fancy' and 'Poems of the Imagination' is not an absolute one: rather, the groups merge into each other, in the middle of an extended scale with purely fanciful and highly imaginative works at the opposite extremes.[1]

In order to introduce the somewhat curious and whimsical mode of these fanciful poems it will be helpful to begin with the second daisy poem, 'With little here to do or see', for this, like so many Romantic and post-Romantic poems, is a poem about writing poetry – in this case a fanciful poem analysing the writing of fanciful poetry.

The poem makes it clear at the outset that the 'grace' of the unassuming daisy arises from a greeting of love by the poet. The second stanza describes the process of composition in detail:

Oft do I sit by thee at ease,
And weave a web of similies,
Loose types of Things through all degrees,
  Thoughts of thy raising:

And many a fond and idle name
I give to thee, for praise or blame,
As is the humour of the game,
   While I am gazing.

That phrase 'weave a web of similies' well describes the effect of these ingenious poems, and 'the humour of the game' sums up their constant playfulness: as the opening lines suggest, they are the work of a man who has consciously withdrawn from the world of affairs.

Wordsworth proceeds to give examples of the sort of unlikely similes which the fancy is prompted to employ on the humble flower; it is a demure nun, a simple sprightly maiden, a fine queen – a waif – deliberately contradictory as one aspect or another of the flower predominates in the observer's mind. This is no longer the obsessive circling movement of the early lyrical ballads, but rather a series of jaunty glances at the flower, snatched impressions. The poet toys with scale, offering in the process an effective delineation of the daisy's appearance, reminiscent of modern 'Martian' poetry:

A little Cyclops, with one eye
Staring to threaten and defy,
That thought comes next – and instantly
   The freak is over,
The shape will vanish – and behold!
A silver Shield with boss of gold,
That spreads itself, some Faery bold
   In fight to cover.

The first comparison is grotesque, suggesting for a moment the latent oddness of the most familiar of objects; the second converts the demure whiteness of the nun to a fairy tale radiance. After such extravagance, the conventional 'star' comparison in the penultimate stanza may seem disappointing, but it is delicately and humorously handled: the daisy is like a star, seen from a distance, but 'Not quite so fair as many are / In heaven above thee!' Nevertheless, the comparison is valid if pressed and reveals a further aspect of the plant:

> Yet like a star, with glittering crest,
> Self-poised in air thou seem'st to rest.

What happens in the remainder of the stanza is indeed disconcerting:

> May peace come never to his nest,
> Who shall reprove thee!

The awkward whimsicality here will strike as absurd even readers who respond to these fanciful poems, so that they find themselves turned into Francis Jeffrey for the nonce. The only thing to be said in its favour, perhaps, is that it alerts one to the most crucial technical development in these 1807 poems: Wordsworth has now three rhymes to find, twice in each stanza, so that the excitement of the rhyming is a major factor in one's response. A comparison with Burns is, as often, instructive. The superiority of Burns's epistles to those by his Ayrshire friends is in no small degree attributable to his rhyming. A tailor's epistle to Burns rhymes conventionally:

> What waefu' news is this I hear,
> Frae greeting I can scarce forbear,
> Folk tells me, ye're gawn aff this year,
>   Out o'er the sea,
> And lasses wham ye lo'e sae dear
>   Will greet for thee.

In reply Burns dashes all such cobwebs away with the vigour and originality of his rhymes:

> What ails ye now, ye lousie b——h,
> To thresh my back at sic a pitch?
> Losh man! hae mercy wi' your natch,
>   Your bodkin's bauld,
> I did na suffer ha'f sae much
>   Frae Daddie Auld.[2]

On the whole, Wordsworth's rhyming tends to be a good deal less vigorous than Burns's at his best, but the reader's eager anticipation and delighted hailing of the third rhyme is still one of the chief pleasures of the 1807 volumes, though at the end of this particular poem it is the second rhyme word ('repair') which is unusual enough to excite a pleasurable sense of surprised recognition, as Wordsworth ends his poem with a humorous reversion to the daisy's unadorned status as 'Flower!' and a delightedly conceived and phrased moral:

> That breath'st with me in sun and air,
> Do thou, as thou art wont, repair
> My heart with gladness, and a share
>   Of thy meek nature!

The first of the daisy poems, 'In youth from rock to rock I went', is much less self-conscious, though in its way equally fanciful. Some of the revisions which Wordsworth introduced, probably in response to Jeffrey's *Edinburgh Review* criticisms, will neatly indicate the boldest and most risky moments in the poem. From 1807 to 1820 the second stanza began:

> When soothed a while by milder airs,
> Thee Winter in the garland wears
> That thinly shades his few grey hairs;
>   Spring cannot shun thee.

That last line was italicised by Jeffrey, presumably to indicate that it was, like the poem in general, 'very flat, feeble, and affected'.[3] Replacing it (in 1827, and again in 1836) entailed a radical reworking of the lines, which finally read:

> Thee Winter in the garland wears
> That thinly decks his few grey hairs;
> Spring parts the clouds with softest airs,
>   That she may sun thee.

In this case it may be felt that the deliberate gaucherie of the original does not pay its way, particularly since the short fourth line is an awkward place to introduce a new season (the similar awkwardness in the following stanza was not eliminated): the revised version is less interesting, but it may be preferred on balance. The fourth line is in both cases a preparation for the fine concluding 'When rains are on thee'. In the third stanza the lively 'If welcome once thou count'st it gain' became more tamely in 1836 'Pleased at his greeting thee again', with a more unambiguous loss. But it is in the second half of the poem that Wordsworth's later discretion wrought most disastrous havoc with fine, bold concepts and expressions. Lines 61–4 originally read:

> At dusk, I've seldom marked thee press
> The ground, as if in thankfulness,
> Without some feeling, more or less,
>   Of true devotion.

This is a charming piece of 'natural piety', and the 'more or less' is not just an infill for the sake of the rhyme, but introduces a self-deprecatory note. The 1815 revision demands a good deal less of the reader:

> And when, at dusk, by dews opprest
> Thou sink'st, the image of thy rest
> Hath often eased my pensive breast
>   Of careful sadness.

Finally, lines 73–6, which were once vigorous and daring:

> Child of the Year! that round dost run
> Thy course, bold lover of the sun,
> And chearful when the day's begun
>   As morning Leveret,

were most sadly bowdlerised in 1836:

> Child of the Year! that round dost run
> Thy pleasant course, – when day's begun
> As ready to salute the sun
>   As lark or leveret.

The vigorous rhyming and the fertility of fancy in the 1807 version of the first daisy poem will repay close scrutiny. Not all of Wordsworth's fanciful flights will be found equally successful, and some readers will fail altogether to respond to the genre. Those who do enjoy poems like this will recognise that Wordsworth has found a new way (or revived a very old way) of celebrating the apparently unremarkable, and of showing that the most vigorous mental powers may find an appropriate and profitable outlet, subduing and fitting high desires to the common world:

If stately passions in me burn,
And one chance look to Thee should turn,
I drink out of an humbler urn
   A lowlier pleasure;
The homely sympathy that heeds
The common life, our nature breeds;
A wisdom fitted to the needs
   Of hearts at leisure.

(49–56)

But such a continuous play of fancy has its perilous side. It can become wearisome to the author, even frightening, as his lively fancy forces upon his retirement myriad images from the world outside, till the actual scene in front of him is eaten up by words and pictures. The danger is strikingly presented in a rare sonnet 'of pure fancy' composed probably between 1802 and 1804:

How sweet is it, when mother Fancy rocks
The wayward brain, to saunter through a wood!
An old place, full of many a lovely brood,
Tall trees, green arbours, and ground flowers in flocks;
And Wild rose tip-toe upon hawthorn stocks,
Like to a bonny Lass, who plays her pranks
At Wakes and Fairs with wandering Mountebanks,
When she stands cresting the Clown's head, and mocks
The crowd beneath her. Verily I think,
Such place to me is sometimes like a dream
Or map of the whole world: thoughts, link by link,
Enter through ears and eyesight, with such gleam
Of all things, that at last in fear I shrink,
And leap at once from the delicious stream.

Two 'Moods of My Own Mind': 'To a Butterfly' *('I've watched you now') and 'I wandered lonely as a Cloud'*

One of the sections in the 1807 volume is headed 'Moods of My Own Mind'. This consists of thirteen very short and varied ejaculations, presented primarily as spontaneous utterances generally less playful, more intense in their joy than the fanciful poems examined above.[4] It is this section that includes the rainbow lyric of spring 1802, an epigraph

100

for much of Wordsworth's most important work:

> My heart leaps up when I behold
>   A Rainbow in the sky:
> So was it when my life began;
> So is it now I am a Man;
> So be it when I shall grow old,
>   Or let me die!
> The Child is Father of the Man;
> And I could wish my days to be
> Bound each to each by natural piety.

Here too is 'The Sparrow's Nest' with its tender and grateful concluding tribute to Dorothy's teaching:

> She gave me eyes, she gave me ears;
> And humble cares, and delicate fears;
> A heart, the fountain of sweet tears;
>   And love, and thought, and joy.

It will be instructive to look at two of these 'Moods' in some detail.

'To a Butterfly', the second poem of that title, has only nineteen lines, but it manages to transport the reader from the orchard at Dove Cottage to the polar regions and from the present to the past, and back again:

> I've watched you now a full half hour,
> Self-poised upon that yellow flower;
> And, little Butterfly! indeed
> I know not if you sleep, or feed.
> How motionless! not frozen seas
> More motionless! and then
> What joy awaits you, when the breeze
> Hath found you out among the trees,
> And calls you forth again!
>
> This plot of Orchard-ground is ours;
> My trees they are, my Sister's flowers;
> Stop here whenever you are weary,
> And rest as in a sanctuary!
> Come often to us, fear no wrong;
> Sit near us on the bough!
> We'll talk of sunshine and of song;

And summer days, when we were young,
Sweet childish days, that were as long
As twenty days are now!

At the core of this poem is one of the most mighty of all Wordsworth's comparisons. The Cyclopean daisy was primarily playful, though it had a serious point to make. The comparison between the butterfly and frozen seas is more like the wave and fountain image in 'The Two April Mornings', but grander and richer. The poem has at its imaginative centre the concept of suspended animation. For half an hour the butterfly has been 'motionless', 'self-poised' on the yellow flower. It will be recalled that in the second daisy poem that flower was 'Self-poised in air' like a star. Wordsworth admires the self-sufficiency, the aplomb of natural objects and, seeking to create a power like one of Nature's, desires that his lyrics be similarly assured, self-poised or (another favourite word) 'steady'. So still is the insect that it might be sleeping or feeding: the process is slightly disconcerting, but not seriously so, for there is no real suggestion here that it might be dead. This arrest is imitated by the repeated exclamation marks after 'motionless' in lines 5 and 6, stopping the movement at the same point, in the same way, in successive lines. The cumulative effect of that comparison should now be apparent: the crinkled surface of the butterfly's wings and the surface of the frozen seas; the expanse of both; the passing impression (since the seas are not seen to unfreeze) of something permanently and totally suspended; the sense of the movement which has been arrested. The joy, elation, and awe compressed into the image make this an astonishingly large-scale, monumental poem. After massive suspension, release is achieved without fuss, with the characteristic assumption that the insect experiences a joy imaging the observer's joy (and the reader's joy in the experience embodied in this stanza). This process is assisted by the natural generosity of the elements: the breeze finding out and calling forth. (The 'f' sound, positioned near the end of lines 1, 2, 4, and 5, has prepared for this breeze, and now comes to the front of line 8 before resuming its accustomed place in line 9.)

The domestic atmosphere of the second stanza comes as a relaxation after the sustained tension and release of the first. Its change in atmosphere is heralded by the conversion of singular flower to plural and the rhyme with 'ours'. Grandeur in Wordsworth is often solitary, remote (the *pathos*). Community is reassuring (the *ethos*), as is possession – though in fact Dove Cottage, like all of Wordsworth's homes till the end of his life, was rented! After the frozen seas, the great intimidating natural processes, there is an orchard plot, a sanctuary, a retreat, in which the creature may be safe. But the poem is to end on a wistful note, returning to the idea of time suspended, in four final lines full of yearning. 'We'll talk' seems to include the butterfly, but when the reader reaches 'when we were young' it is clear that the human participants are talking to each other, and that their human consciousness of time is placing a barrier between themselves and the natural world. They remember 'Sweet childish days': 'childish' is habitually used by Wordsworth in a non-pejorative sense and always in a context of regret; in particular it recalls here the first 'To a Butterfly' at the beginning of the 'Moods of My Own Mind' series, where the creature brings to mind the 'Dead times' when 'in our childish plays / My Sister Emmeline and I / Together chaced the Butterfly!' The poem concludes subtly with an extension of the first stanza by one penultimate line, quietly reinforcing the sense (the additional rhyme word is 'long') and adding a final firmness to a remarkably strong and finely conceived structure.

The other 'Mood' to be considered closely is the familiar 'I wandered lonely as a Cloud'. There are two major problems with this poem. In the first place it exists in two versions, as published in 1807 and 1815, and in this case (as with *The Prelude*) each has serious claims to critical attention. The 1807 version will form the basis of this discussion, and the 1815 addition and alterations will be considered at the end. The other problem is one of familiarity. (At a gathering in London to raise funds for Dove Cottage a recitation of this poem is reported to have reduced the audience to fits of laughter, confirming Wordsworth's low estimation of metropolitan audiences.) With the veil of familiarity removed, the opening should be astonishing. Wordsworth is fond of

1807 version

I wandered lonely as a Cloud
That floats on high o'er Vales and Hills,
When all at once I saw a crowd
A host of dancing Daffodils;
Along the Lake, beneath the trees,
Ten thousand dancing in the breeze.

The waves beside them danced, but they
Outdid the sparkling waves in glee:—
A Poet could not but be gay
In such a laughing company:
I gazed – and gazed – but little thought
What wealth the shew to me had brought.

For oft when on my couch I lie
In vacant or in pensive mood,
They flash upon that inward eye
Which is the bliss of solitude,
And then my heart with pleasure fills,
And dances with the Daffodils.

---

cloud comparisons, for their sense of isolated and stately progression.[5] Here there is a sense of floating into a vale, seeing the daffodils suddenly, as it were on rounding a crag. The first chapter noted the importance for this poem of a scrupulously careful reading, so as to observe the dancing of waves and daffodils and eventually of the poet's heart in retrospective delight. When it is carefully read, the piece is a near-perfect exemplification of Coleridge's description of the 'secondary imagination' in the *Biographia Literaria*: 'it struggles to idealize and to unify. It is essentially *vital*, even as all objects (*as* objects) are essentially fixed and dead.'[6] In a

1815 version

> I wandered lonely as a cloud
> That floats on high o'er vales and hills,
> When all at once I saw a crowd,
> A host, of golden daffodils;
> Beside the lake, beneath the trees,
> Fluttering and dancing in the breeze.
>
> Continuous as the stars that shine
> And twinkle on the milky way,
> They stretched in never-ending line
> Along the margin of a bay:
> Ten thousand saw I at a glance,
> Tossing their heads in sprightly dance.
>
> The waves beside them danced: but they
> Out-did the sparkling waves in glee:
> A poet could not but be gay,
> In such a jocund company:
> I gazed – and gazed – but little thought
> What wealth the show to me had brought:
>
> For oft, when on my couch I lie
> In vacant or in pensive mood,
> They flash upon that inward eye
> Which is the bliss of solitude;
> And then my heart with pleasure fills,
> And dances with the daffodils.

---

particular pensive mood, a mood of the poet's own mind, the past-outward is made present-inward, the heart fills with pleasure and beats in sympathy with the recollected universal dance.

Geoffrey Durrant has made an eloquent case for the more elaborate four-stanza version of the poem published in 1815.[7] He points out that the wealth at the end of the third stanza in 1815 (corresponding to the second in 1807) is enriched by the substitution of 'golden' for 'dancing' in the fourth line, and he praises the expansive milky way image. Yet, as so often, there is loss as well as gain, and the 1807 version may be more fully appreciated when the nature of this loss is recognised. The 'golden' in line 4 means that the repeated 'dancing' in lines 4 and 6 disappears, and (rather worse) that the echo in 'laughing' at line 10 is changed to 'jocund', which disrupts the poem's music. The final 'dances' in the last line depends for much of its effect on this sound patterning: 'dancing', 'dancing', 'danced', 'laughing', 'dances', and the echoing of 'daffodils'. To sacrifice this is to lose much of the characteristic music and vitality of the poem. It may also be felt that the 'wealth' is adequately prepared by the 'Ten thousand', and that the force of 'Along the lake' is not recaptured in the final version's 'Beside the lake' and 'Along the margin of a bay'. Whatever conclusion is reached, the process of comparison is educative and should make it clear that popularity need not be despised: this is a remarkably fine poem.

Two domestic poems: 'Louisa' and 'She was a Phantom of delight'

The lines in 'The Sparrow's Nest' paying tribute to Dorothy were noted above, and no doubt in one sense most of Wordsworth's poems about girls or young women are partly inspired by her. The recent publication of Wordsworth's love letters has surprised some readers into a recognition that he also loved his wife, and with a lover's love. The 1807 volume contains two great love poems – 'Louisa', which probably refers to Dorothy, and 'She was a Phantom of delight', a poem about Mary Wordsworth which should have alerted such readers to the depth of the married relationship. Both of these are among the finest love poems in the language.

'Louisa' has a superb opening line: 'I met Louisa in the shade'. Many of Wordsworth's poems at this period grip the reader by virtue of the definitive, strange, haunting character of their openings:

Among all lovely things my Love had been

Behold her, single in the field

106

I travelled among unknown Men

I wandered lonely as a Cloud

In youth from rock to rock I went

Look, five blue eggs are gleaming there!

Loud is the Vale! the Voice is up

She was a Phantom of delight

There was a roaring in the wind all night

Where lies the Land to which yon Ship must go?

With Ships the sea was sprinkled far and nigh.

The first line of 'Louisa' was actually replaced in 1836 by a very badly conceived revision, but Wordsworth thought better in 1845. The magnificent vigour of the last three lines of the stanza was sacrificed in the same revision. The original reads:

> Why should I fear to say
> That she is ruddy, fleet, and strong;
> And down the rocks can leap along,
> Like rivulets in May?

The word 'ruddy' was too rude for 1836, when it became 'healthful', and in 1845 it further metamorphosed to 'nymph-like', which totally misses the point of this country vigour.

Wordsworth reserves the unearthly side of Dorothy for the delicate play of words in the second stanza, and the sensuous side of his affection (which is not to suggest anything excessive) for the third. The final stanza is the most complex, introducing the device, increasingly common in the later work, of quotation from a classic text:

> Take all that's mine 'beneath the moon,'.

The phrase in quotation marks is Shakespearian, from *King Lear* and (possibly) *Antony and Cleopatra*. In *King Lear* it occurs as Edgar (disguised as Mad Tom) is conducting his blind father Gloucester to Dover and making him imagine that they are at the top of a cliff:

Give me your hand; you are now within a foot
Of the extreme verge: for all beneath the moon
Would I not leap upright.

(IV. iv. 26–8)

In *Antony and Cleopatra* Cleopatra's speech on Antony's death ends: 'there is nothing left remarkable / Beneath the visiting moon' (IV. xiii. 67–8). It is difficult to know how far such references ought to be pressed. The *King Lear* passage may have come to mind partly because of the leaping of Louisa, and perhaps a hint of the secrecy and distancing of blindness is cast retrospectively over the second stanza where her smiles 'as they pass away, / Are hidden in her eyes'. There may also be a sense of protectiveness, of the essential fragility of even this strong woman, as she performs her daring feats. As for the Cleopatra aspect of the reference (Shakespeare's phrasing is slightly different, and it may not have been in Wordsworth's mind at all), it might, as in 'Beggars', introduce a sunburnt Egyptian grandeur to add to Louisa's other endowments. It might also suggest that the narrator, observing Louisa from the shade which recalls the opening, is (compared with her vitality) dead as Antony is dead, spell-bound, ready to give up a world for her. The lines recall Marvell's exquisite 'Let me be laid, / Where I may see thy Glories from some shade'.[8] The sense of fragility, of mortality, introduced by the quotation is particularly poignant in view of Dorothy's later mental illness. One recalls that, like Louisa, the Idiot Boy was associated with a waterfall.

Something of the same combination of robust earthiness and rare spirituality can be found in the poem inspired by Mary Wordsworth, 'She was a Phantom of delight'. The first distant view of early acquaintance is allowed to occupy the opening stanza, whose idealisations possess a validity beyond the mere ornament of a moment. Lines 5 and 8 lend Mary something of a goddess's abundant majesty:

Her eyes as stars of Twilight fair;
Like Twilight's, too, her dusky hair;
But all things else about her drawn
From May-time and the cheerful Dawn.

But the lines also correspond to Mary's actual appearance, and the witty, daring final word of the stanza keeps the thing from becoming too solemn. She is an abstraction, a 'dancing Shape', an 'Image gay', but a cheerful one, her haunting beneficent, herself something amazing – trapping the speaker unaware, but for his own good.

The second stanza does not deny what has been gleaned from first impressions, but finds the purely earth-bound Mary equally forceful. Wordsworth delicately maintains a little of the spiritual aura in lines 13 and 14:

> Her household motions light and free,
> And steps of virgin liberty.

The second line might have occurred in a poem about the goddess Diana. As part of the constantly fresh and varied approach, Mary's face is next seen as a sort of legal document, but a wholly unforbidding one:

> A countenance in which did meet
> Sweet records, promises as sweet.

'Sweet' is not one of Wordsworth's notable words (his handling of it tends to lack subtle shades of meaning),[9] and he rightly eliminated a good many occurrences in revision, but here it effectively dispels any trace of the formidable.

The final stanza begins with an extraordinary couplet:

> And now I see with eye serene
> The very pulse of the machine.

De Selincourt has a note citing *inter alia* Hamlet's use of 'machine' for his body, and a passage from a book familiar to Wordsworth, Bartram's *Travels*: 'At the return of the morning, by the powerful influence of light, the pulse of nature becomes more active, and the universal vibration of life insensibly and irresistibly moves the wondrous machine.'[10] Wordsworth does not use the word in this sense elsewhere, and it must have been as odd for him as for his readers. Bartram's sense is most apposite here, the 'wondrous machine', the extraordinary working together of body and spirit with the pulse of life, anticipating the 'nobly planned' of line 27. There is one further striking line, 'A Being breathing thoughtful breath': Wordsworth often uses the noun 'being' to explore the mystery and wonder of existence human, animal, vegetable, and divine, and a similar range is covered by the rich words 'breath' and 'breathe'.[11] The poem ends firmly but more conventionally – especially after 1845 when 'an angel light' became 'angelic light', depriving the last line of a slight twist. After such a poem the couple's love letters should not have come as a surprise.

Several other fine domestic poems in the 1807 collection can be recommended – notably the quietly joyful 'Among all lovely things my Love had been', the tender but fearful Marvellian 'To H.C., Six Years Old', and above all the gravely wounded poem about Coleridge's disaffection 'A Complaint'. All of these, if read aloud and given time to breathe, will make their various telling effects.

Four Scottish poems: 'The Solitary Reaper', 'Yarrow Unvisited', 'Glen Almain', and 'The Matron of Jedborough and her Husband'

The Wordsworths' tour of Scotland in 1803 resulted in a fascinating group of poems which introduce elements new to his work.

'The Solitary Reaper' centres on two of these innovations, one conceptual, the other technical. This is a prime example of what Geoffrey Hartman has termed Wordsworth's 'poetry of surmise'. When something is uncertain (in this case the girl is singing in Gaelic, so that Wordsworth cannot know what she sings) then the poet's imagination can have freedom of surmise.[12] Without surmise, indeed, this poem would hardly exist. The music is free to impress the reader as it had the narrator, initially in a superb couplet at the end of the first stanza:

> O listen! for the Vale profound
> Is overflowing with the sound.

(Dorothy Wordsworth found 'something inexpressibly soothing to me in the sound of those two Lines . . . I often catch myself repeating them in disconnection with any thought, or even, I may say, recollection of the Poem.')[13]

This immersion in sheer sound suggests two of Wordsworth's finest imaginative expansions by way of comparison. The first converts the Highland vale to an oriental
oasis, the girl's voice to a nightingale's song, and the
narrator (and his presumed companions) to a band of desert
travellers. The second simile is no less magical, though
located nearer home and ornithologically precisely accurate.
It may be noted that this stanza greatly benefited in revision
in 1827 and afterwards by the elimination of both 'sweetly'
and 'sweeter' in lines 10 and 13 (the second and fifth lines
below). The final version reads:

> No Nightingale did ever chaunt
> More welcome notes to weary bands
> Of travellers in some shady haunt,
> Among Arabian sands:
> A voice so thrilling ne'er was heard
> In spring-time from the Cuckoo-bird.
> Breaking the silence of the seas
> Among the farthest Hebrides.

That crucial substituted 'thrilling' in line 13 makes it clear
that there is no lack of emotional power in the girl's song.
Geoffrey Finch well remarks: 'The suspension of activity
which he experiences is reached not through lack of emotion
but through the very force of it. Aesthetic experience, the
poem implies, is at its deepest level the moment when the
urge for identity is held against the sense of separateness.'[14]
His uncertainty leads the narrator to speculate throughout
the third stanza as to the subject of the song, with wistful
romantic effect. The words may refer either to old public
sorrows or to everyday unspectacular personal losses. Just as
Wordsworth's genius is being applied to the everyday, so
the act of song can be equally impressive – not irrespective
of subject (the matter is clearly not comic, for example), but
over a wide range of subjects of varying degrees of
importance in conventional estimation. In the girl's singing,
as often happens in Wordsworth, time is suspended: 'the
Maiden sang / As if her song could have no ending'. One
recalls the butterfly, 'motionless . . . motionless', and there is
the same contrast with vast time-scales. In order to suggest
this suspension of time Wordsworth makes repeated use of

the present participle suffix '-ing'. It chimes throughout, both as suffix and as part of the root: 'single', 'Reaping', 'singing', 'sings', 'overflowing', 'Nightingale', 'thrilling', 'spring-time', 'Breaking', 'sings', 'things', 'ending', 'singing', 'bending'. This sound echoes in the mind after reading the poem, along with the three-foot fourth line. The solitary reaper's song has truly no ending.

Surmise is even more crucial in 'Yarrow Unvisited', but it is of a different sort and touches on a question which was always central in Wordsworth's thinking. The river Yarrow is celebrated in Scottish song, and the headnote to the poem actually makes reference to these songs and quotes from one of them to start the half-playful sequence of rhymes on 'Yarrow':

(See the various Poems the scene of which is laid upon the Banks of the Yarrow; in particular, the exquisite Ballad of Hamilton, beginning

'Busk ye, busk ye my bonny, bonny Bride,
Busk ye, busk ye my winsome Marrow!' –)

The speaker and his own 'winsome Marrow' discuss whether or not to visit the river, and in urging that they should continue their journey without seeing it the narrator finds himself forced into an extreme position:

'What's Yarrow but a River bare
That glides the dark hills under?
There are a thousand such elsewhere
As worthy of your wonder.'

(25–8)

This extreme reduction poses the challenge of a radical scepticism about landscape. To what extent is our appreciation the result of conditioning by our predecessors? Without history (as Scott would argue) and without art, what is Yarrow 'but a River bare'? But to speak thus is for Wordsworth akin to blasphemy, and as narrator he is shocked to hear the words coming from his mouth:

– Strange words they seemed of slight and scorn;
My True-love sighed for sorrow;
And looked me in the face, to think
I thus could speak of Yarrow!

He happily concedes the tradition by quoting from Hamilton's ballad (35) and by mentioning two attractive details gleaned, in fact, from Scott during their stay with him at Ashestiel:

'Let Beeves and home-bred Kine partake
The sweets of Burn-mill meadow;
The Swan on still St. Mary's Lake
Float double, Swan and Shadow!'

Those last two lines owe their luminous quality to an artistic refinement which Scott did not usually share to the same extent. In quoting them in a note to his fascinating but very different medieval narrative poem *Marmion* he made them read:

The swans on sweet St Mary's lake
Float double, swan and shadow.

Wordsworth pointed out the error rather than letting it pass in silence,[15] for like Sir George Beaumont's friend in the case of 'I wandered lonely as a Cloud' Scott has quite missed the point, here the haunting effect of the single swan on the still lake, swan and shadow. With such tradition and such second-hand detail combining to make up a visionary picture, the narrator now argues, it would be foolish to expect the river itself to be in any way adequate to their expectations:

'Enough if in our hearts we know,
There's such a place as Yarrow.'

(47–8)

Somewhat inconsistently, but probably with psychological truth, he ends by suggesting that if in future their travelling days are done the thought of the unvisited stream will be a consolation to them, when their dreams of the unseen are unlikely to be tested against reality. The argument of this poem is a penetrating one, and it may be viewed as a minor but attractive gloss on the crossing of the Alps in *The Prelude*.

As striking reminders of the two poles of Wordsworth's power – extreme peace and extreme energy, the former never without intensity in his best work, the latter never without a final repose – attention is claimed by two somewhat neglected but very remarkable poems from the Scottish set, 'Glen-Almain' and 'The Matron of Jedborough'.

Wordsworth's love of secluded vales has been encountered more than once in this study. Seclusion means retreat and peace, but it also comes close to death, and that closeness may produce either a deeper peace or an unease. In the 1800 *Lyrical Ballads* Wordsworth had published a strange, haunting fragment later called 'The Danish Boy',[16] about an eerily secluded moorland spot, a dell avoided by birds and bees, where the shadow or spirit of a harping boy sings alone. Like the solitary reaper's, his song is ambiguous; like the girl whom Matthew encounters in 'The Two April Mornings' he has a stony face, and his stillness is akin to that of a corpse:

> There sits he; in his face you spy
> No trace of a ferocious air,
> Nor ever was a cloudless sky
> So steady or so fair.
> The lovely Danish Boy is blest
> And happy in his flowery cove:
> From bloody deeds his thoughts are far;
> And yet he warbles songs of war,
> That seem like songs of love,
> For calm and gentle is his mien;
> Like a dead Boy he is serene.
>
> (45–55)

'Glen-Almain' is a poem of a similar extreme, unearthly quiet, taking its cue from the reputed burial of Ossian, the ancient Gaelic heroic poet, in the 'Narrow Glen'. 'Narrow' seems to have set Wordsworth on a minimalist line of thinking. The first section of the poem is straightforward, with a scrupulous noting of the inappropriateness of such a burial place for a poet of violent action, for 'this is calm; there cannot be / A more entire tranquillity' (15–16). As in 'The Danish Boy' and elsewhere in Wordsworth the word 'calm' has visionary overtones,[17] and in the second part of this poem the thought develops in a strangely disquieting direction. The piece begins with a play, of the sort often associated with the grave, on the word 'groundless':

Does then the Bard sleep here indeed?
Or is it but a groundless creed?

The belief that Ossian is buried here may have no earthly
foundation: it would then be a human fancy, but this raises
the stranger question as to why such a spot should have
been considered appropriate. Wordsworth conjectures that
the inventors of the story wished thus to give expression to
their feeling for the spot, much as he (and perhaps the sea-
captain and his informants) had elaborated the story
associated with 'The Thorn'. His reason for this conjecture
is at the heart of the poem:

> A Convent, even a hermit's Cell
> Would break the silence of this Dell:
> It is not quiet, is not ease;
> But something deeper far than these:
> The separation that is here
> Is of the grave; and of austere
> And happy feelings of the dead:
> And, therefore, was it rightly said
> That Ossian, last of all his race!
> Lies buried in this lonely place.

The notion of something that goes beyond peace, an
intensity so great that in it extremes of passion and quiet
meet, is a remarkable one. To express it, Wordsworth takes
a word which he has made his own, 'quiet', and denies it in
the interests of something quieter than quietness, something
that is both 'happy' (not at all a superficial word here) and
austere.

'The Matron of Jedborough and Her Husband' is one of
Wordsworth's most daring poems. Like 'Glen-Almain' it is
both joyful and disturbing, but in a very different way. It is
made clear early in the poem that the husband is a hopeless
cripple, and it is strongly suggested in the penultimate
stanza that his wife is unstable, quite apart from her own
physical handicaps:

> I looked, I scanned her o'er and o'er;
> The more I looked I wondered more:
> When suddenly I seemed to espy
> A trouble in her strong black eye;

115

A remnant of uneasy light,
A flash of something over-bright!
And soon she made this matter plain;
And told me, in a thoughtful strain,
That she had borne a heavy yoke,
Been stricken by a twofold stroke;
Ill health of body; and had pined
Beneath worse ailments of the mind.

That stanza comes as a shock after the previous joyous negations of helplessness. (The opening adjuration to Age to dance is, with a fine decorum, reminiscent of Burns's personifications at the beginning of 'The Holy Fair'.) The husband's physical decrepitude, too, is not underestimated:

With legs that move not, if they can,
And useless arms, a Trunk of Man,

(16–17)

and he is likened in a striking comparison to one who 'breathes a subterraneous damp' (26), and to the now silent tower of ruined Jedburgh Abbey. Wordsworth is drawing here on his early experience of Cockermouth Castle, summed up in a sonnet of 1833, 'Address from the Spirit of Cockermouth Castle':

Erewhile a sterner link
United us; when thou, in boyish play,
Entering my dungeon, didst become a prey
To soul-appalling darkness. Not a blink
Of light was there; – and thus did I, thy Tutor,
Make thy young thoughts acquainted with the grave.

(5–10)

Immobile, silent, acquainted like the young Wordsworth with the grave, the Jedburgh man is at first sight the exact opposite of his wife 'in the prime of glee' (9), her lamp 'bright as Vesper' (27) like Jedburgh itself in its heyday (29–33). The narrator heaps praise on the wife – heroic, with a well-spent life behind her, strong, and above all defying old age by living with the utmost vigour to the end:

Our Human-nature throws away
Its second Twilight, and looks gay:

116

> A Land of promise and of pride
> Unfolding, wide as life is wide.
>
> (44–7)

With great delicacy Wordsworth charts the minimal but vital contact between husband and wife, and with a moving touch he introduces a triplet to describe the motions of the couple's eyes, recalling the dancing triplet at the end of the first stanza (the only other in the poem, sadly eliminated in a revision of 1827):

> Utterly dead! yet, in the guise
> Of little Infants, when their eyes
> Begin to follow to and fro
> The persons that before them go,
> He tracks her motions, quick or slow.
> Her buoyant Spirit can prevail
> Where common cheerfulness would fail:
> She strikes upon him with the heat
> Of July Suns; he feels it sweet;
> An animal delight though dim!
> 'Tis all that now remains for him!
>
> (52–62)

The 'heat / Of July Suns' is a peculiarly intense form of the 'spring' and 'May' awakening of lines 1 and 33, the husband's response an 'animal' one; yet such is Wordsworth's scrupulosity that the minimal nature of the joy is reiterated even at this high moment: "tis all that now remains for him!'

After this, the penultimate stanza quoted above is totally unexpected. The narrator 'seemed to espy / A trouble': it is a conjecture, but one which is to be confirmed by the matron's speech. In the face of his disclosure, the narrator is still bold enough to see her present vitality as 'a second Spring' and secure enough to end with a thanksgiving. After so intense an experience, such an ending comes as a welcome relief.

The Scottish poems also contain the spirited 'Rob Roy's Grave', a poem disconcerting in a different sense. Wordsworth's admiration for Rob's reliance on natural instinct as against law is a development of the 1798 lyrics, but the

attempt to make Rob an anti-Napoleonic leader, a beneficent power, is a good deal less comforting than Wordsworth evidently intends it to be. From his retreat Wordsworth begins to write public poetry in these years, most
notably in the sonnets, to which attention now turns.

The Sonnets

Most modern readers who approach Wordsworth's sonnets
will do so out of a sense of duty. In the course of a long life
he wrote an inordinate number, many on public themes
such as 'Confirmation Continued' and capital punishment
(of which he somewhat reluctantly approved, for murder).
Most of them are very dull; but some of the 1807 public
sonnets (the majority gathered under the heading 'Sonnets
Dedicated to Liberty') are of interest, and the more private
sonnets in the same publication (headed 'Miscellaneous
Sonnets') include at least two outstanding examples of the
genre.[18]

Wordsworth's view of the form was made clear in a very
satisfactory prefatory sonnet composed, according to Jared
Curtis, 'perhaps around late 1802':[19]

> Nuns fret not at their Convent's narrow room;
> And Hermits are contented with their Cells;
> And Students with their pensive Citadels:
> Maids at the Wheel, the Weaver at his Loom,
> Sit blithe and happy; Bees that soar for bloom,
> High as the highest Peak of Furness Fells,
> Will murmur by the hour in Foxglove bells:
> In truth, the prison, unto which we doom
> Ourselves, no prison is: and hence to me,
> In sundry moods, 'twas pastime to be bound
> Within the Sonnet's scanty plot of ground:
> Pleased if some Souls (for such there needs must be)
> Who have felt the weight of too much liberty,
> Should find short solace there, as I have found.

This is an intensely personal statement. Wordsworth is
attracted to the sonnet as one of those souls who 'have felt
the weight of too much liberty'. It will be remembered that

although he composed exquisitely crafted miniatures at this period he was also engaged in writing *The Prelude*, a work entirely without the discipline of external form. The burden of that responsibility must have weighed heavily. The sonnet is for Wordsworth and his readers a salutary traditional discipline, though one accepted only for brief periods and 'in sundry moods'.

A much later sonnet, dating probably from 1826, and published as a dedicatory poem prefixed to the Miscellaneous Sonnets in 1827, begins with nine lines summing up Wordsworth's formal desideratum:

> Happy the feeling from the bosom thrown
> In perfect shape (whose beauty Time shall spare
> Though a breath made it) like a bubble blown
> For summer pastime into wanton air;
> Happy the thought best likened to a stone
> Of the sea-beach, when, polished with nice care,
> Veins it discovers exquisite and rare,
> Which for the loss of that moist gleam atone
> That tempted first to gather it.

Wordsworth was most attracted to the Miltonic form of the sonnet, with its avoidance of firm divisions, either of the Shakespearian 4 + 4 + 4 + 2 variety or the Petrarchan 8 + 6, as he explained in a letter written in the spring of 1833 to Alexander Dyce:

It should seem that the Sonnet, like every other legitimate composition, ought to have a beginning, a middle, and an end – in other words, to consist of three parts, like the three propositions of a syllogism, if such an illustration may be used. But the frame of metre adopted by the Italians does not accord with this view, and, as adhered to by them, it seems to be, if not arbitrary, best fitted to a division of the sense into two parts, of eight and six lines each. Milton, however, has not submitted to this. In the better half of his sonnets the sense does not close with the rhyme at the eighth line, but overflows into the second portion of the metre. Now it has struck me, that this is not done merely to gratify the ear by variety and freedom of sound, but also to aid in giving that pervading sense of intense Unity in which the excellence of the Sonnet has always seemed to me mainly to consist. Instead of looking at this composition as a piece of architecture, making a whole out of three parts, I have been much in the habit of preferring the image of an orbicular body, – a sphere – or a dew-drop. All this will appear to you a little fanciful; and I am well aware that a Sonnet will often be found excellent, where the beginning, the middle, and the end are distinctly marked, and also where it is distinctly separated into *two* parts, to which, as I have before observed, the strict Italian model, as they write it, is favorable.[20]

Wordsworth's ideal, then, is an organic whole in which the feeling of a moment will crystallise into a fourteen-line form, filling the space available precisely, and indeed his three-part blueprint is rarely to be as clearly discerned as in the fine early sonnet 'Calm is all nature as a resting wheel'. Where there is a division, it is most likely to be between octave and sestet, following the Petrarchan form. One of the better 'Sonnets Dedicated to Liberty' (No. 3, 'Jones! When from Calais southward you and I') is a case in point, though it spoils the effect in its last two lines almost as badly as a number of Shakespeare's sonnets with their awkward concluding couplets. Although this set of sonnets has some fine phrases ('man's unconquerable mind' at the end of No. 8, 'To Toussaint L'Ouverture', for example) the overall impression is of the cool performance of a public duty. Thus No. 6, 'On the Extinction of the Venetian Republic', quite lacks the incandescent quality of Byron or Shelley when they write about Venice (or of Turner when he paints it). Perhaps the most interesting aspect of these 'Liberty' sonnets is their insistence that public figures should value highly their domestic life, that there should be no scorning of the ordinary. This is summed up in one nicely epigrammatic line from No. 4, 'I grieved for Buonaparte': 'Wisdom doth live with children round her knees' (9), and it is one of the chief themes of probably the finest of this group, No. 14, 'London, 1802', whose distinctly separated sestet reads:

> Thy soul was like a Star and dwelt apart:
> Thou hadst a voice whose sound was like the sea;
> Pure as the naked heavens, majestic, free,
> So didst thou travel on life's common way,

In chearful godliness; and yet thy heart
The lowliest duties on itself did lay.

The theme recurs in the once much admired poem 'Character of the Happy Warrior':

> – He who, though thus endued as with a sense
> And faculty for storm and turbulence,
> Is yet a Soul whose master-bias leans
> To home-felt pleasures and to gentle scenes;
> Sweet images! which, wheresoe'er he be,
> Are at his heart; and such fidelity
> It is his darling passion to approve;
> More brave for this, that he hath much to love.

(57–64)

It may be that the disciplined carefulness of this poem and the 'Liberty' sonnets will come into their own again in public esteem. For the moment most readers will pay a distant tribute and pass to the 'Miscellaneous Sonnets'.

Three very different sonnets of high quality represent Wordsworth's command of this difficult form at its most assured. Miscellaneous Sonnet No. 14, 'Composed Upon Westminster Bridge, Sept. 2, 1802', has been the subject of much analysis. Presuming that the sonnet has been read in the normal direction, it may conveniently be analysed in reverse. Wordsworth is conscious of London as a metropolitan heart, through which the life of the land circulates, and which is almost suspended in sleep. (J. Hillis Miller takes 'still' to have overtones of death here, and though 'still' would more naturally in this context mean 'at a low level of activity', or at most 'in suspended animation', Wordsworth's habitual association of extreme quiet with death lends support to the argument.)[21] It will by now come as no surprise that Wordsworth particularly values this extreme calm which recalls (in negative comparison) the rising sun steeping 'valley, rock, or hill': that word 'steep' catches the early morning sun and the sense of the sunlight sinking into the moist bracken on the fells. The city is assimilated to the natural world of Wordsworth's own home, so that the Thames seems almost a country river, a Derwent perhaps:

121

The river glideth at his own sweet will.

The provincial admiration of the city may also be discerned in the octave in a curious use of words:

> Dull would he be of soul who could pass by
> A sight so touching in its majesty.

'Touching . . . majesty' suggests tenderness and grandeur, but one may also detect a submerged echo of the touching for the King's Evil, the healing by laying on of hands which English sovereigns practised: James VI of Scotland and I of England adopted it on assuming the joint throne in 1603, and it survived into the reign of Queen Anne. (The practice is familiar from *Macbeth* and from Boswell's *Life of Johnson*.)[22] Wordsworth as another northern provincial comes to London, paradoxically to see and feel a calm deeper than he has ever felt before. Metropolitan hands are laid on him, that his soul may not be dull, but they are curiously familiar.

Perhaps the best commentary on this sonnet is a parallel experience of the metropolis which Wordsworth records in a letter to Sir George Beaumont of 8 April 1808:

> I left Coleridge at 7 o'clock on Sunday morning; and walked towards the City in a very thoughtful and melancholy state of mind; I had passed through Temple Bar and by St Dunstan's, noticing nothing, and entirely occupied with my own thoughts, when looking up, I saw before me the avenue of Fleet street, silent, empty, and pure white, with a sprinkling of new-fallen snow, not a cart or Carriage to obstruct the view, no noise, only a few soundless and dusky foot-passengers, here and there; you remember the elegant curve of Ludgate Hill in which this avenue would terminate, and beyond and towering above it was the huge and majestic form of St Pauls, solemnised by a thin veil of falling snow. I cannot say how much I was affected at this unthought-of sight, in such a place and what a blessing I felt there is in habits of exalted Imagination. My sorrow was controlled, and my uneasiness of mind not quieted and relieved altogether, seemed at once to receive the gift of an anchor of security.[23]

Miscellaneous Sonnet No. 16, 'Methought I saw the footsteps of a throne', presents a type of vision very rare in Wordsworth. (The Arab Quixote at the beginning of Book V of *The Prelude* is another example.) One thinks immediately of Keats, and no doubt the vision of Moneta in *The Fall of Hyperion* was influenced in part by this haunting poem. The sombre vision of the 'miserable crowd', and the wholly unexpected sleeper in the mossy cave, sleeping and dead or perhaps as if dead, fill octave and sestet perfectly. The word 'ruefullest' stands out, possibly a nonce-word, as unusual a coinage for Wordsworth as the vision itself. The 'throne' rhyme echoes throughout the sonnet, culminating in the ambiguous 'forgone' ('passed away', 'gone before', or 'dispensed with') which qualifies 'a thought' (a particular thought, or thinking itself). The 'summer' of the final line is one of the most heart-stopping placings of a common word in all of Wordsworth.

This poem is further enriched by a companion sonnet composed in November 1836 and placed after it in 1837. Sara Hutchinson, Mary's sister, had especially loved that sestet, and when she died Wordsworth looked on her face in the light of the sonnet. The 1836 poem is a conventional piece, but it adds a telling personal comment:

> Even so for me a Vision sanctified
> The sway of Death; long ere mine eyes had seen
> Thy countenance – the still rapture of thy mien –
> When thou, dear Sister! wert become Death's Bride:
> No trace of pain or languor could abide
> That change:— age on thy brow was smoothed – thy cold
> Wan cheek at once was privileged to unfold
> A loveliness to living youth denied.
> Oh! if within me hope should e'er decline,
> The lamp of faith, lost Friend! too faintly burn;
> Then may that heaven-revealing smile of thine,
> The bright assurance, visibly return:
> And let my spirit in that power divine
> Rejoice, as, through that power, it ceased to mourn.

The finest of all the sonnets, and one of the noblest ever written, is Miscellaneous Sonnet No. 18. This is a private statement, but the subject is one that also occurs several times in the 'Liberty' sequence – the deadening commercialism of current British society. It is the main subject of 'Liberty' Sonnets Nos 17, 'When I have borne in memory', and 20, 'These times touch moneyed Worldlings with dismay', and it appears also in No. 14, 'London, 1802'. This commercialism of early nineteenth-century Britain permeates the first four lines of No. 18:

> The world is too much with us; late and soon,
> Getting and spending, we lay waste our powers:
> Little we see in nature that is ours;
> We have given our hearts away, a sordid boon!

The two opening words refer to the world of affairs, but there is also probably a biblical and Prayer Book sense of the world as opposed to the life of the spirit. To give away the heart is usually an act of love, but here it is poisoned by overtones of commercial transactions: it has been given as a bribe or a sweetener, a 'sordid boon'. The result of all the commercial activity and bribery has been that, unnoticed, what is most truly and valuably 'ours' (the world of 'nature', here referring primarily to the external natural world) has ceased to be so.

By the time that one moves on to the second half of the octave in a Petrarchan sonnet one is eager to discover in which direction the rhymes will take the sense. Here the 'soon' / 'boon' rhyme leads to 'moon' and 'tune' – the first involving a reference to the inward mutuality of the natural world from which we are now cut off by our neglecting of our powers:

> This Sea that bares her bosom to the moon.

The 'tune' in 'For this, for every thing, we are out of tune' is not a wholly new image introduced awkwardly for the rhyme but has been prepared by the 'howling' of the two previous lines which have had to take up the 'powers'/'ours' rhyme:

> The Winds that will be howling at all hours
> And are up-gathered now like sleeping flowers.

That 'all hours' links with the nightscape of the previous line, and the simile is a perfect example of the way in which

exigencies of rhyme have led to a daring expansion of
thought, here in the reverse direction to that observed in
'The Two April Mornings' or the butterfly poem, compar-
ing the vast with the tiny, tenderly accommodating the
howling winds to the sea, presumably calm, baring her
bosom to the moon.

The second half of the octave spills over into the sestet for
two feet, to good effect, and it is followed by one of
Wordsworth's noblest endings, whose evocation of the
splendours of Greek mythology makes one regret that as a
rule, in reaction against cold and routine classicising, he
tended to avoid the area. The influence of this sonnet on
Keats (compare 'On First Looking into Chapman's Homer')
must again have been profound. Three details contribute to
the effect. Proteus 'coming' became in 1827 'rising', but the
first version is grander in its generality, as Wordsworth's
uses of the verb 'to be' are usually more impressive than
specific later substitutes. In the last line the disyllabic
'wreathèd' adds a crucial antique touch (one remembers the
'kissèd' towards the end of 'Michael'). All this is seen from a
'pleasant lea', the bland adjective acquiring a strange force
from the noun extracted from its centre. Finally the intensity
of the poem is centred in a set of sexual and related images.
The sea bares her bosom, the speaker would rather be 'A
Pagan suckled in a creed outworn' than unmoved by
Nature, and the commercial imagery of the opening lines is
also capable of sexual interpretation, commercialism being a
disastrous type of sublimation, as war is in Byron's *Don
Juan*.

The Miscellaneous Sonnets include other successes, or
partial successes. One of these, No. 19, 'It is a beauteous
Evening, calm and free', which has an impressive octave, is
an imaginative link between the Miscellaneous and 'Liberty'
Sonnets, the point of connection being the English Channel.
Wordsworth's mind often reverted to the Channel because
of Annette Vallon and their daughter, Caroline. In 1802,
during the Peace of Amiens, he and Dorothy met them at
Calais on the eve of his marriage. The political sonnets make
much of Calais, Dover, and the Channel between, and here
the infusion of personal feeling adds an imaginative lustre to
sometimes rather undistinguished public material.

Three stoical poems: 'Resolution and Independence', 'Peele Castle' ('Elegiac Stanzas'), and the Immortality Ode

It is a measure of the variety of the 1807 volumes that they should include both the poems of fancy and three immensely grave, elevated pieces which rise as great mountain peaks in Wordsworth's *oeuvre*.

The opening two lines of 'Resolution and Independence' immediately indicate that this is to be a poem on the grand scale and one of great seriousness:

> There was a roaring in the wind all night;
> The rain came heavily and fell in floods.

Thus, as it were, Wordsworth inscribes '*serioso*' at the head of his poem, as Beethoven was soon to denominate his Op. 94 string quartet, '*quartetto serioso*'. The alternation between fierce storm and the calm morning which has succeeded establishes the manic-depressive atmosphere of the work. Wordsworth begins in the present with two introductory stanzas, and from a 'pleasant' morning full of self-sufficient but ephemeral life echoing through its 'chatters . . . waters . . . glittering' casts his thought back to a similar 'pleasant' season when he had experienced that sudden reversion of spirit which afflicts many people of high talent capable of extreme delight – those 'blind' thoughts which may not be altogether understood or easily resisted. Some of Wordsworth's most cherished words come in for questioning. The narrator is 'a happy Child of earth', whose perpetual childhood is now rudely disrupted. He had lived his life 'in pleasant thought', as if it were 'a summer mood', in 'genial faith, still rich in genial good'. The experience leads him to moral considerations: he has been irresponsible, has taken too much for granted the labours of others (40–2). This moral questioning assumes a weight equal to the 'fate of poets' motif in the seventh stanza:

> I thought of Chatterton, the marvellous Boy,
> The sleepless Soul that perished in its pride;
> Of Him who walked in glory and in joy
> Behind his plough, upon the mountain-side:

126

By our own spirits are we deified;
We Poets in our youth begin in gladness;
But thereof comes in the end despondency and madness.

The encounter with the leech-gatherer which helps the poet-narrator to find a firmer faith, to endure more resolutely and in a more sustained manner, may have come about 'by peculiar grace' (50), both adjective and noun being religious terms: certainly it was not of his conscious seeking. The description of the old man is elemental. In a fine 1820 revision he stands 'Beside a Pool bare to the eye of Heaven' (cf. 54); in all versions he is 'a Man', and 'The oldest Man he seemed that ever wore grey hairs'. Wordsworth himself explained the effect of the comparisons with stone and sea-beast in a brilliant observation in his 'Preface to the Edition of 1815':

> In these images, the conferring, the abstracting, and the modifying powers of the Imagination, immediately and mediately acting, are all brought into conjunction. The Stone is endowed with something of the power of life to approximate it to the Sea-beast; and the Sea-beast stripped of some of its vital qualities to assimilate it to the stone; which intermediate image is thus treated for the purpose of bringing the original image, that of the stone, to a nearer resemblance to the figure and condition of the aged Man; who is divested of so much of the indications of life and motion as to bring him to the point where the two objects unite and coalesce in just comparison. After what has been said, the image of the Cloud need not be commented upon. (Gill, p. 633)

The narrator characteristically sees in the ambiguous state between life and death something both disturbing and potentially calming, but here there is a grotesque comedy in the man's physical embodiment of 'extreme old age':

His body was bent double, feet and head
Coming together in their pilgrimage.

(73–4)

The following three lines speak of human convulsions akin to the geological as the man is akin to stone, which is in turn akin to sea-beast:

> As if some dire constraint of pain, or rage
> Of sickness felt by him in times long past,
> A more than human weight upon his frame had cast.

The old man stood 'Upon the margin of that moorish flood', this 'margin' and perhaps the constraints of rhyme leading to his conning the water 'As if he had been reading in a book'. It may be that Wordsworth means simply to suggest great absorption as the man seeks out his leeches, but it may also be that he wishes to draw attention to the oral nature of the dialogue that follows. He seeks to understand, by questioning, a secret imaged in the silent intercourse between reader and book, particularly if the book is in a language not understood by the observer.

Wordsworth handles the dialogue carefully, letting the reader hear only a limited amount, and it is not until near the end that one learns what the man's actual words were.[24] The narrator's first remark is neutral, no more than a passing of the time of day; the man's reply is gentle, courteous, slow, and presumably equally noncommittal, but sufficiently attractive in manner to lead to a sympathetic question:

> 'What kind of work is that which you pursue?
> This is a lonesome place for one like you.'
>
> (95–6)

The 1820 revision of the first of those lines, to read 'What occupation do you there pursue?', might suggest that the original is close to the actual words which Wordsworth might have used on such an occasion, but the words of the reply are not recorded, and even its gist – hardship, resignation to God's will, usefulness – given in the stanza beginning at line 99 is subordinated to the further description of the leech-gatherer's manner of speaking:

> He answered me with pleasure and surprize;
> And there was, while he spake, a fire about his eyes.
>
> His words came feebly, from a feeble chest,
> Yet each in solemn order followed each,
> With something of a lofty utterance drest;
> Choice word, and measured phrase; above the reach
> Of ordinary men; a stately speech!

128

Such as grave Livers do in Scotland use,
Religious men, who give to God and Man their dues.

It is clear that no stranger has been interested in this man before (there is probably an implicit 'Simon Lee'-like rebuke to the readers), and the contrast between the feeble utterance and the perceived strangeness – the solemn, lofty, deliberate, stately speech – is a telling one. Wordsworth remembers the gist of the man's speech when composing the poem, but at the time of the encounter the words melted into one of those *Ursprachen*, elemental pre-linguistic noises, going deeper than words, though Wordsworth has only words with which to suggest them (one recalls the foreign languages of the Highland Reaper and the Emigrant Mother). So he resorts to analogy. The old man's voice was 'like a stream / Scarce heard'; his 'whole Body . . . did seem / Like one whom I had met with in a dream'; he is like a man sent to strengthen him – or to exorcise an evil spirit. For the spirit of dejection bids fair to rend the poet-narrator as it is forced out of him, the language intense and deeply earnest:

> My former thoughts returned: the fear that kills;
> The hope that is unwilling to be fed;
> Cold, pain, and labour, and all fleshly ills;
> And mighty Poets in their misery dead.
>
> (120–3)

At this point the 1820 version of line 117, a typical filling-in with explanatory detail of the sort so common in *The Prelude*, is more helpful than obtrusive:

> – Perplexed, and longing to be comforted,
> My question eagerly did I renew,
> 'How is it that you live, and what is it you do?'

That first, altered, line rings true in the situation: it is the apparently strong man who is in the greater need. (One notes that for the renewed question, even though the form is altered, Wordsworth repeats the rhyme of lines 88 and 89.) The leech-gatherer's reply is specific, and it is at this point that his words are first quoted. They are wholly unremarkable in themselves: Wordsworth's point is presumably that on the page the words are dull, but read with the feelings that he has attempted to describe they are revelatory of extraordinary, heroic endurance – an endurance which, in that favourite word, 'troubled' his hearer with a vision of total loneliness, and, since nobody speaks to him, total silence. The cheerfulness and the stateliness in one whose profession parallels his own (providing healing, and diminished from past glories) lead to a sense of proportion, and a final exclamation which is banal only if the reader still finds the old man's quoted words unmoving.[25]

Wordsworth had need of fortitude, for in January 1805 his beloved brother John, captain of the *Earl of Abergavenny*, went down with his ship off Weymouth. The second of the three great stoical poems is Wordsworth's most moving and impressive elegy for his brother, though it is cast in the form of a merciless, perhaps too merciless, self-examination. The full title is 'Elegiac Stanzas, Suggested by a Picture of PEELE CASTLE, in a storm, *painted* by Sir George Beaumont'.

In the first half of the poem Wordsworth recalls his summer holiday in 1794 and talks of its cheerful mood as a delusion. He is in fact suggesting that much of his previous life has been a slumber akin to that in the first stanza of 'A slumber did my spirit seal'. It 'seemed no sleep' (9) while the etherialised 'Form' of the rugged castle 'was sleeping on a glassy sea' (the reference being presumably to the heavenly sea of glass of Revelation 4:6 and 15:2). It also seemed 'no mood', but something permanent, and many of Wordsworth's most cherished words are enlisted to suggest the attractiveness of that deluded time: pure sky, quiet air, perfect calm, gentleness. The summer seemed timeless (6), the image of the castle, in a play on words, ever present and ever 'still' (7); yet the picture is shot through with hints of the disaster to come. The image 'trembled' on the water (8); there was seeming, fancying: 'The light that never was, on sea or land' is a miracle or an illusion. The idealised painting that Wordsworth wished to produce would have depicted the castle 'Amid a world how different from this', a paradisal, Elysian, and possibly unreal world where the castle would have seemed 'a chronicle of heaven', a story of the beyond time, or in temporal terms 'a mine / Of peaceful years' which would be exempt from human sorrows. 'No motion but the moving tide' ominously recalls the very different 'No motion has she now, no force' of 'A slumber did my spirit seal'.

When in the central stanza the idealised picture has been regretfully dismissed as 'the fond delusion of my heart' (29), Wordsworth introduces his chastened view of a possible future life at once more disciplined and more human. But just as in the first half of the poem the ideal had been constantly qualified, so now in the course of preferring the new realism he has to admit to a substantial loss of 'power', a loss which one suspects may have contributed to his poetic decline ('power' is one of Wordsworth's more complex terms, but it is often used to denote poetic or visionary capability):[26]

> A power is gone, which nothing can restore.
>
> (35)

What follows is moving, but disquieting. He speaks 'with mind serene' (40), but the serenity comes from a numbness, a diminution in intensity, an insulation from feeling, as becomes clear in the third last stanza:

> And this huge Castle, standing here sublime,
> I love to see the look with which it braves,
> Cased in the unfeeling armour of old time,
> The light'ning, the fierce wind, and trampling waves.

The 'trampling waves' are intense enough, the passionate work ('work' is a powerful word), and the rueful sky recalling that 'ruefullest' in the sonnet on death, 'Methought I saw the footsteps of a throne'. But the farewell to the heart that lives alone is a farewell to the heart of his own imaginative being: blindness has not usually been a pejorative term in Wordsworth, as it is here; the 'fortitude' is genuine, but the 'hope' is a diminished one.

The radical ambiguities and uncertainties of this poem add to its deeply moving effect, as a magnificent fierce sunset, a raging against the dying of the light.

The poem headed simply 'Ode' which concludes the 1807 volumes had been completed in 1804, the year before 'Peele Castle'. In 1815 Wordsworth gave it the expanded title 'Ode: Intimations of Immortality from Recollections of Early Childhood', and it is generally known as the

Immortality Ode. It has stood at the end of most complete editions of Wordsworth, following his own example, and it is right that it should have done so; for although it is in two important respects untypical of his work, it places his creative endeavours in a new context, and in spite of adverse criticisms which parts of it have attracted it is a very fine poem indeed, possibly the finest he ever wrote.

The Ode is untypical firstly in being an ode at all. Although the term has few formal implications in the period – this one is in irregular stanzas, which rhyme and scan freely – the generic title does imply a degree of willed grandeur and elevation which might be thought to be alien to Wordsworth's genius. In fact, although Coleridge objected to 'mental bombast' in part of the work, Wordsworth succeeds in marrying the most extreme simplicity ('The things which I have seen I now can see no more', l. 9) with an effective elevation of style and image. The elevation is typified by the line 'The Cataracts blow their trumpets from the steep' (125). That is clearly not a straightforward comparison, since cataracts do not sound in the least like trumpets. There is an aural element (the noise is grand and inspiriting), but the metaphor is as much visual: the cataracts pour water from the steep as waves from a trumpet-like aperture, or like visual representations of the waves of sound. As for Coleridge's accusation of 'mental bombast' in the ninth stanza (108ff), Wordsworth means to be provoking in his claims for the child, and his meditation at this point is of such uncomfortable profundity that even Coleridge could not bear it.

The concept underlying the poem is also thoroughly untypical of Wordsworth, for it is one of the very few works of his to employ a mythological base. In talking to Isabella Fenwick towards the end of his life he was careful to stress that the myth of pre-existence is not to be taken as a formal doctrine. Rather closer to the date of the poem's composition, in January 1815, he remarked in a letter to Mrs Clarkson:

> This poem rests entirely upon two recollections of childhood, one that of a splendour in the objects of sense which is passed away, and the other an indisposition to bend to the law of death

132

as applying to our own particular case. A Reader who has not a vivid recollection of these feelings having existed in his mind in childhood cannot understand that poem.[27]

One contemporary who responded favourably to the Ode was William Blake. In general Blake regarded Wordsworth as an apostate of the imagination, and when he read the 'Prospectus' to *The Recluse* (which appears as the final section of 'Home at Grasmere') the experience is said to have brought on a bowel complaint which nearly killed him. The lines which he particularly objected to were these:

> I, long before the blessed hour arrives,
> Would sing in solitude the spousal verse
> Of this great consummation, would proclaim –
> Speaking of nothing more than what we are –
> How exquisitely the individual Mind
> (And the progressive powers perhaps no less
> Of the whole species) to the external world
> Is fitted; and how exquisitely too –
> Theme this but little heard of among men –
> The external world is fitted to the mind.
>
> (1002–11)

As Geoffrey Hartman above all has pointed out, Wordsworth's imagination had a strong apocalyptic element, though in his work there is at least as pronounced an impulse to see imagination and world as fitting, to demonstrate that Grasmere contains in itself a sufficiency for the most vital mind to work with. The Immortality Ode is certainly, along with parts of *The Prelude*, Wordsworth at his most apocalyptic. The young child wishes to 'fit his tongue / To dialogues of business, love, or strife' (97–8), and while that would be generally disapproved of in any Wordsworth poem there is a wider horror at the personified Earth in the sixth stanza (resembling Blake's mildly but efficiently repressive Enitharmon, which Wordsworth would not have known):

> Earth fills her lap with pleasures of her own;
> Yearnings she hath in her own natural kind,
> And, even with something of a Mother's mind,
>   And no unworthy aim,

The homely Nurse doth all she can
To make her Foster-child, her Inmate Man,
Forget the glories he hath known,
And that imperial palace whence he came.

(77–84)

The earth is 'natural', and the associated word 'kind' spreads
from its immediate meaning 'sort' into 'kindness', 'kinship'.
As Lionel Trilling showed in a classic essay,[28] the 'glories' of
pre-existence which Earth tries to make her foster-child
forget are part of a dominant stream of imagery connected
with light. The child is born accompanied by sunrise
splendour, or glory (which means 'light' or 'halo' in one of
its senses); the splendour soon fades into the light of
common day; the poet learns to accept this with regret and
to appreciate both natural dawn as an image of the departed
spiritual glory and the more sober splendours of sunsets:

The innocent brightness of a new-born Day
Is lovely yet;
The Clouds that gather round the setting sun
Do take a sober colouring from an eye
That hath kept watch o'er man's mortality.

(197–201)

The 'celestial light' which in Wordsworth's youth apparelled
every human sight (1–4) is the 'consecration', the 'poet's
dream' which 'Peele Castle' was to view more sceptically in
1805. Here its loss is deeply regretted, though in the first
four stanzas (composed in 1802) this regret is expressed as a
lyric utterance without the mythological framework developed in the resumed ode in 1804. The poet is isolated in his
grief from the springtime rejoicing, which is stylised and
made exotic: 'tabor' is archaic and oriental (21); 'jubilee' (38)
is 'general rejoicing', 'the sound of rejoicing', but with
overtones of the Hebrew *yobel* ('ram' and 'ram's horn')
linking with the cataracts' trumpets and the shepherd boys;
'coronal' ('circlet') two lines below was almost as exotic in
Wordsworth's time as it is today. If one is right in thinking
that the 'timely utterance' which gave Wordsworth relief
was 'My heart leaps up' (quoted in part from 1815 onwards
as epigraph to the Ode), then this adds a further point to the
spirited line 'And the Babe leaps up on his mother's arm'

(49). Although the poet is temporarily absorbed into this festivity 'While the Earth herself is adorning' (43), there is a hint of emotion being worked up, or of an odal repetition being too easily assumed: 'I feel – I feel it all', 'I hear, I hear, with joy I hear!' As with the repeated 'happy's in the third stanza of Keats's ode 'On a Grecian Urn' the hint of falsity may be strategic, here preparing for the recurrence of depression:

> – But there's a Tree, of many one,
> A single Field which I have looked upon,
> Both of them speak of something that is gone:
>> The Pansy at my feet
>> Doth the same tale repeat:
> Whither is fled the visionary gleam?
> Where is it now, the glory and the dream?

Wordsworth is recalled from ecstatic or would-be ecstatic general rejoicing by the individual tree or field, and it is with the specific that he ends the poem:

> To me the meanest flower that blows can give
> Thoughts that do often lie too deep for tears.

After the intervening meditation he is able to approach the single tree, or field, or flower with a subdued but continuing confidence that they will suffice.

Centring on the mythological machinery of the poem is a set of profoundly disturbing images often associated in Wordsworth's mind: sleep, blindness and sensory deprivation, blankness, haunting, and death. These are just as important as the pervasive light image with which they interweave an unsettling counterpoint. The first hint of that importance comes in the haunting line in the third stanza 'The Winds come to me from the fields of sleep' (28). The winds sleep on the fields; they leave the fields sleeping; they come from the world of sleep as inspiring breezes: these and other appropriate responses are all invited. Then at the beginning of the resumed ode and the mythological meditation Wordsworth writes: 'Our birth is but a sleep and a forgetting', where 'sleep' is more ominous and negative, our life apparently so full of activity being seen as a mere sleep, presumably without 'the freshness of a dream' (5), rather with the hackneyed 'dream of human life' adopted by the child (91). It is clear that by 1804 Wordsworth has moved into a still more radically unsettling world than that of two years earlier. This becomes especially apparent in the eighth stanza, which incurred Coleridge's disapproval:

> Thou best Philosopher, who yet dost keep
> Thy heritage, thou Eye among the blind,
> That, deaf and silent, read'st the eternal deep,
> Haunted for ever by the eternal mind.
>
> (110–13)

The child reads eternity like a book. Adults hear and speak, but they are blind. The child sees, but cannot hear and cannot (or will not) speak: presumably he is, at his visionary height, deaf to the world's 'dialogues' of the previous stanza and silent because he cannot analyse or express in speech his innate vision. But in his decline, 'yet glorious' (124), he fails to see the light, 'Thus blindly with thy blessedness at strife'. Adult life is also conceived of as a burial under a crushing load:

> Full soon thy Soul shall have her earthly freight,
> And custom lie upon thee with a weight,
> Heavy as frost, and deep almost as life!
>
> (129–31)

The child in his prime regards death and literal burial as a bleak but temporary state, in lines which Coleridge understandably found too fearsome, and which Wordsworth deleted in 1820:

> To whom the grave
> Is but a lonely bed without the sense or sight
> Of day or the warm light,
> A place of thought where we in waiting lie.
>
> (120–3)

The blankness of the grave has here overcome for a moment the positivity of the child's attitude, and indeed the image immediately preceding it is almost as unsettling:

> Thou, over whom thy Immortality
> Broods like the Day, a Master o'er a Slave,
> A Presence which is not to be put by.
>
> (117–19)

The child's haunting can be a fearful thing, its deafness and silence intimidating, its vision of death remorselessly literal as in 'We are Seven', just as its earnest intentness on conforming to adult life has the force of a rush of lemmings. The reason for this ominous dislocation becomes clear in the next stanza as Wordsworth gives thanks

> for those obstinate questionings
> Of sense and outward things,
> Fallings from us, vanishings;
> Blank misgivings of a Creature
> Moving about in worlds not realized,
> High instincts, before which our mortal Nature
> Did tremble like a guilty Thing surprized.
>
> (144–50)

The apocalyptic vision is glorious, but it is also terrible.[29] It has power to 'make / Our noisy years seem moments in the being / Of the eternal Silence' (156–8), its deaf and dumb prophet reading the text of an eternal being akin to not-being.

The new image of the sea which ends the central section of the Ode (164–70) is very grand, but for all its oceanic sense it falls short of making the deeps of eternity wholly attractive to humanity. It is no wonder that one feels with Wordsworth a sense of relief at a now unforced rejoicing in 'the May', in the sacramental habitual joy, rather than in contemplation of the deep truth which, as Shelley's Demogorgon says with some justification, is imageless.[30] The whole of human endeavour, of history, is enlisted to place Wordsworth's meditation in perspective in what for this reader is among the most moving lines in all of English poetry:

> Another race hath been, and other palms are won.
>
> (202)

Gerard Manley Hopkins wrote:

There have been in all history few, a very few men, whom
common repute, even where it did not trust them, has treated
as having had something happen to them that does not
happen to other men, as having *seen something*, whatever that
really was. Plato is the most famous of these. Or to put it as
it seems to me I must somewhere have written to you or to
somebody, human nature in these men saw something, got a
shock; wavers in opinion, looking back, whether there was
anything in it or no; but is in a tremble ever since. Now what
Wordsworthians mean is, what would seem to be the
growing mind of the English speaking world and may
perhaps come to be that of the world at large / is that in
Wordsworth when he wrote that ode human nature got
another of those shocks, and the tremble from it is spreading.
This opinion I do strongly share; I am, ever since I knew the
ode, in that tremble.[31]

CHAPTER 5

Conclusion

Looking back in 1823, Wordsworth believed that as a young man 'I had full as much of the poetic Spirit in me as I have ever had since', but that it was not 'untill my 28th year [1796–97], though I wrote much, that I could compose verses which were not in point of workmanship very deficient and faulty'.[1] That '28th year' had heralded his stylistic coming of age in 'The Ruined Cottage' and the *Lyrical Ballads*, but there is much to enjoy in the comparatively derivative earlier poems. *An Evening Walk* and *Descriptive Sketches* may be 'juvenile productions, inflated and obscure, but they contain many new images, and vigorous lines':[2] the close observation in the former and moments of glowing and brooding grandeur in the latter will impress some modern readers as they did Coleridge. 'Salisbury Plain' is notable for its invocation of a weird spirit of place, and Wordsworth's unique tragedy *The Borderers*, though hovering uneasily between stage and closet, has powerfully apocalyptic moments and some intriguing analytical psychology.

After completing *The Prelude* in 1805 and publishing the *Poems, in Two Volumes* in 1807, Wordsworth suffered the fatal loss of energy discussed in the first chapter, and most of his voluminous later poetry is a faded sepia recollection of, or commentary upon, the work of the great decade. He could still be roused to greatness, most often by the subject of death: the sonnets 'Surprised by Joy' and 'On the Departure of Sir Walter Scott', the gravely classical 'Laodamia', and the 'Extempore Effusion Upon the Death of James Hogg' are especially noteworthy elegiac master-pieces. His attempt to etheralise Scott's narrative poetry in *The White Doe of Rylstone* is partly successful, and *The Excursion* contains fine narrative and meditative passages, notably the account of classical mythology in Book IV (687–881) which profoundly influenced Keats. Gill's selection of the best short poems from the last forty-five years is a good starting point for exploring the later work.

John Wordsworth once remarked: 'Most of William's poetry improves upon 2nd 3rd or 4th reading.'[3] Whatever the merits of the early and late periods, for the majority of readers it is the poems of 1798–1807 that will attract repeated attention, for these have the indispensable ability of the greatest work to come up fresh and to astonish on each perusal. At the heart of this achievement is Wordsworth's skill in placing ordinary words in such combinations as may reveal new facets of well-worn terminology. Readers should not be misled by the strongly mimetic and expressionist standpoint adopted in the Preface to *Lyrical Ballads* into imagining that Wordsworth neglected poetry as a craft. His letters and his notes to individual poems show the finest regard for workmanship: the Preface omits such considera-tions because he takes it for granted that a serious poet will attend rigorously to them. Only the most scrupulous craftsmanship could have resulted in the sustaining tensions which Coleridge observed in his work and subsequently applied more generally:

> It was not . . . the freedom from false taste, whether as to
> common defects, or to those more properly his own, which
> made so unusual an impression on my feelings immediately,
> and subsequently on my judgement. It was the union of deep
> feeling with profound thought; the fine balance of truth in
> observing with the imaginative faculty in modifying the
> objects observed; and above all the original gift of spreading
> the tone, the *atmosphere*, and with it the depth and height of
> the ideal world around forms, incidents, and situations, of
> which, for the common view, custom had bedimmed all the
> lustre, had dried up the sparkle and the dew drops.[4]

To expand on Coleridge's list: Wordsworth's finest poems hold in daring tension humour and seriousness, delicacy and

Conclusion

strength, tenderness and grandeur, the subjective and the
objective, the intellect and the emotions, energy and repose.
They appeal immediately to a wide range of readers and
have remained unexhausted by many thousands of critical
interpretations.

It would be wrong to overemphasise the limitations of
Wordsworth's subject matter, for the poems of his prime are
remarkably varied. His concentration on his own mind in
The Prelude is of the greatest interest as part of a revolution
in consciousness (having its immediate origin in seventeenth-
century spiritual autobiography and eighteenth-century
psychological investigations) which had revealed the importance of the observer's contribution to all perception and the
complexity of the individual mind. But the poetry of the
great decade is equally concerned with the fundamental
human passions as observed quasi-scientifically in a variety
of mostly rural characters, in the relationship between
humankind and the natural world, and in public affairs.
Wordsworth recognised that 'the range of poetic feeling is
far wider than is ordinarily supposed, and the furnishing
new proofs of this fact is the only *incontestible* demonstration
of genuine poetic genius'.[5] His own revolutionary explora-
tions of the common and unexotic show the same passionate
scrupulosity that determines his way with words, as he
seeks to educate his readers in 'the pathos of humanity',[6] the
dignity of all humankind, and proper loving relationships
among people and between people and their environment,
'whole continents of moral sympathy':[7]

> I attach no interest to my poems in their connection with the
> world further than as I think they are fitted to communicate
> knowledge, to awaken kindly or noble dispositions, or to
> strengthen the intellectual powers; in a word to promote just
> thinking and salutary feelings. . . . If my Poems are inspired
> by Genius and Nature they will live, if not, they will be
> forgotten and the sooner the better.[8]

Readers who respond to this challenge will find in
Wordsworth's greatest work an abiding and constantly
increasing pleasure, and many will surely experience a
response similar to that of the Quaker bank clerk Bernard
Barton, to whom Wordsworth wrote in 1816:

141

It pleases, though it does not surprize me, to learn that, having been affected early in life by my verses, you have returned again to your old Loves after some little infidelities, which you were shamed into by commerce with the scribbling and chattering part of the World. I have heard of many who, upon their first acquaintance with my poetry, have had much to get over before they could thoroughly relish it; but never of one who, having once learned to enjoy it, had ceased to value it or survived his admiration. This is as good an external assurance as I can desire that my inspiration is from a pure source, and that my principles of composition are trustworthy.[9]

Abbreviated References

Averill   James H. Averill, *Wordsworth and the Poetry of Human Suffering* (Ithaca, NY, and London, 1980).

Beer   John Beer, *Wordsworth and the Human Heart* (London and Basingstoke, 1978).

Biographia   S.T. Coleridge, *Biographia Literaria*, ed. James Engell and W. Jackson Bate, 2 vols (Princeton, NJ, and London, 1983).

Brett and Jones *Lyrical Ballads*, ed. R.L. Brett and A.R. Jones (London, 1963).

Clarke   C.C. Clarke, *Romantic Paradox: An Essay on the Poetry of Wordsworth* (London, 1962).

Curtis   *'Poems, in Two Volumes', and Other Poems, 1800–1807*, ed. Jared Curtis (Ithaca, NY, 1983).

de Selincourt   *The Prelude*, ed. Ernest de Selincourt, 2nd edition, rev. Helen Darbishire (Oxford, 1959).

Gill   *William Wordsworth*, ed. Stephen Gill (Oxford and New York, 1984) (The Oxford Authors).

Hartman   Geoffrey Hartman, *Wordworth's Poetry: 1787–1814* (New Haven, Conn., and London, 1964).

Havens   Raymond Dexter Havens, *The Mind of a Poet: A Study of Wordsworth's Thought*

	with Particular Reference to 'The Prelude' (Baltimore, Md, 1941).
Letters	*The Letters of William and Dorothy Wordsworth*, ed. Ernest de Selincourt (2nd edition, Oxford, 1967–).
Jones	John Jones, *The Egotistical Sublime: A History of Wordsworth's Imagination* (London, 1954).
Perkins	David Perkins, *Wordsworth and the Poetry of Sincerity* (Cambridge, Mass., 1964).
Poetical Works	*The Poetical Works of William Wordsworth*, ed. Ernest de Selincourt and Helen Darbishire, 5 vols (Oxford, 1940–9).
Prose	*The Prose Works of William Wordsworth*, ed. W.J.B. Owen and Jane Worthington Smyser, 3 vols (Oxford, 1974).
Ricks	Christopher Ricks, *The Force of Poetry* (Oxford, 1984).
Roper	*Lyrical Ballads 1805*, ed. Derek Roper, 2nd edition (Plymouth, 1976).
J. Wordsworth	Jonathan Wordsworth, *William Wordsworth: The Borders of Vision* (Oxford, 1982).

Notes

1 *Introduction*

1   William Hazlitt, 'My First Acquaintance with Poets': *Complete Works of William Hazlitt*, ed. P.P. Howe, 21 vols (London and Toronto, 1930–4), XVII, 117. Thomas De Quincey, letter to Wordsworth, 31 May 1803: John E. Jordan, *De Quincey to Wordsworth: A Biography of a Relationship* (Berkeley and Los Angeles, 1963), p. 30. John Wilson, letter to Wordsworth, 24 May 1802: Brett and Jones, p. 333.

2   Curtis, pp. 330–1.

3   *Letters*, II, 194–5 (c. 20 February, 1808).

4   See, for example, the very detailed emendations of the 1800 *Lyrical Ballads* sent to the printer: *Letters*, I, 311–12.

5   Byron, *Don Juan*, III, 94.

6   In a letter to Thomas Manning [late February 1801]: *The Letters of Charles Lamb to which are added those of his sister Mary Lamb*, ed. E.V. Lucas, 3 vols (London, 1935), I, 251.

7   *Journals of Dorothy Wordsworth*, ed. Mary Moorman (Oxford, 1971), p. 117. For a more ambiguous moment a week earlier see 'These chairs they have no words to utter', Gill, p. 255.

8   Blake, *The Marriage of Heaven and Hell*: 'The Voice of the Devil'.

9   *Letters*, I, 543: [12 February] 1805.

10 Averill, pp. 90–1.

11 John Jones, writing of Wordsworth's solitaries: Jones, p. 68.

12 *Edinburgh Review*, 11 (October 1807), 214–31.

13 *Letters*, IV, 600n, 640.

14 'Simon Lee, the Old Huntsman', 83; 'To the Daisy' ('In youth

from rock to rock I went'), 17; 'Tintern Abbey', 106; 'I
travelled among unknown Men', 6.

15   Coleridge exaggerated when he said in a letter to Robert
Southey that 'Wordsworth's words always *mean* the whole of
their possible Meaning' (14 August 1803: *Collected Letters of
Samuel Taylor Coleridge*, 6 vols (Oxford, 1956–71), II, 977),
but it is a pardonable over-statement. At the heart of
Wordsworth's poetic achievement is an exploration of the
richness which certain common words possess, and a
development of his own characteristic range of significances.
A Wordsworth glossary would show how he explores many
of the peculiar resonances of a limited number of favoured
words, such as: alone, along, being, blank, blind, blood,
blooming, breath(e), calm, cloud, common, course, darkness,
deep, delight, desire, dream, dreary, drink, dull, earth, eye,
face, faith, fancy, far, fear, feed, feel, fit, fix, flash, fond,
form, frame, gaze, genial, gentle, ghastly, grace, hang, heart,
hollow, hope, imagination, impress, impulse, joy, law,
lead, lie, life, light, line, love, mind, mood, moral, motion,
naked, nature, nook, passion, peace, pleasure, power,
presence, quiet, reason, region, roll, season, seem, sense,
serene, service, silence, single, soul, spirit, spread, steady,
stir, thing, think, touch, trouble, truth, voice, waters, weight,
and word.

16   Roger N. Murray, *Wordsworth's Style: Figures and Themes in
the 'Lyrical Ballads' of 1800* (Lincoln, Nebr., 1967), p. 13.

17   F.J. Hugo, 'Wordsworth's Perception of Unity and
Diversity', *Theoria*, 52 (May 1979), 50–62 (p. 58).

18   See for this and many other examples Christopher Ricks,
'William Wordsworth 2: "A sinking inward into ourselves
from thought to thought"': Ricks, pp. 117–34.

19   Arnold, 'Stanzas in Memory of the Author of "Oberman"',
53–4; Byron, *Don Juan*, I, v.

20   *Letters*, II, 264: 4 August [1808].

21   See the excellent article by L.J. Swingle, 'Wordsworth's
Contrarieties: A Prelude to Wordsworthian Complexity',
ELH, 44 (1977), 337–54 (p. 345).

22   *Letters*, I, 234; II, 222–3.

23   *Prelude*, III, 124–9.

24   *Biographia*, I, 80 (chapter 4).

25   See Helen Sard Hughes, 'Two Wordsworthian Chapbooks',

Modern Philology 25 (1927–28), 207–10, and *Letters*, II, 248.

26 See, for example, 'Home at Grasmere', 1001, and *Prelude*, I, 118.

27 Local resident quoted by H.D. Rawnsley, *Literary Associations of the English Lakes*, 2 vols (Glasgow, 1901), II, 136–8.

28 'The Tables Turned', 21.

29 'To Joanna', 38–40; 'Fidelity', 25–6 (not in Gill); 'A whirl-blast', 13–14.

30 David McCracken, *Wordsworth and the Lake District: A Guide to the Poems and Their Places* (Oxford, 1984).

31 See Russell Noyes, *Wordsworth and the Art of Landscape* (Bloomington, Ind., and London, 1968), and Ken Lemmon, 'Poet's Hand on the Landscape: Wordsworth's Garden at Rydal Mount, Cumbria', *Country Life*, 175 (3 May 1984), 1240–2.

32 See especially [John Murdoch], *The Discovery of the Lake District: A Northern Arcadia and Its Uses* (London: Victoria and Albert Museum, 1984).

2 *Lyrical Ballads* (1798 and 1800)

1 *Critical Review* (Second Series), 24 (October 1798), 197–204: quoted in Brett and Jones, pp. 319–20.

2 *Monthly Review* (New Series), 29 (June 1799), 202–10: quoted in Brett and Jones, p. 321.

3 *British Critic*, 14 (October 1799), 364–9: quoted in Brett and Jones, pp. 323–6. For the tentative identification see Derek Roper, *Reviewing before the 'Edinburgh'* (London, 1978), p. 283 n. 77. By '*Darwinian*' is meant the inflated style of the contemporary scientist-poet Erasmus Darwin.

4 For sources of quotations see Chapter 1 n. 1.

5 See the classic article by R.D. Mayo, 'The Contemporaneity of the *Lyrical Ballads*', *PMLA*, 69 (1954), 486–522.

6 'Mr Wordsworth', in *The Spirit of the Age: Complete Works of William Hazlitt*, ed. P.P. Howe, 21 vols (London and Toronto, 1930–4), XI, 87.

7 For a different assessment see Andrew L. Griffin, 'Wordsworth and the Problem of Imaginative Story: the Case of "Simon Lee"', *PMLA*, 92 (1977), 392–409 (pp. 399–400).

8 See Brett and Jones, p. 284.

9   W.J.B. Owen sees Wordsworth's encounter with the thorn as
    a 'spot of time' akin to those described in *The Prelude*: ' "The
    Thorn" and the Poet's Intention', *Wordsworth Circle*, 8 (1977),
    3–17 (p. 15).

10 Walt Whitman's phrase is applied to the poem by Averill (p.
    172). Averill's discussion includes an important consideration
    of the narrator as a ghoul taking a morbid delight in his tale
    of another's suffering.

11 See 'spot syndrome' in the index to Hartman.

12 *Poetical Works*, II, 514.

13 *Poetical Works*, II, 478.

14 In a fine essay Angus Easson suggests that the muses refuse
    the narrator full knowledge of romance: 'Apparently the
    narrator/poet has a high idea of poetry as something able to
    open magic casements, a power for the wonders of fiction,
    whereas the poem seems to say poetry's purpose is to come to
    some understanding of reality' (' "The Idiot Boy":
    Wordsworth Serves out his Poetic Indentures', *Critical
    Quarterly*, 22:3 (1980), 3–18 (p. 15).

15 *Poetical Works*, II, 478.

16 Stephen K. Land comments: 'Johnny's simplicity, like that of
    many Wordsworthian children, isolates him from linguistic
    contamination and preserves his experience inviolate from
    secondary associations and verbal intentions. In this way his
    two lines of nonsense suggest a realm of necessarily
    incommunicable poetry' ('The Silent Poet: An Aspect of
    Wordsworth's Semantic Theory', *University of Toronto
    Quarterly*, 42 (1973), 157–69 (p. 167).

17 See Thomas M. Helmstader, 'Wayward Wisdom:
    Wordsworth's Humor in the *Lyrical Ballads*', *Mosaic*, 9:4
    (Summer 1976), 91–106 (p. 97).

18 J.R. Watson, *Wordsworth's Vital Soul: The Sacred and Profane in
    Wordsworth's Poetry* (London and Basingstoke, 1982), pp.
    152–5.

19 For the concept of the 'one life' see 'The Ruined Cottage',
    218, *Prelude*, II, 430, and Jonathan Wordsworth, *The Music of
    Humanity* (London, 1969): 'One Life' in index.

20 Roper, pp. 320–1.

21 Jonathan Ramsey suggests that the weather-cock
    appropriately suggests instability, and that it is 'a fragment of
    a much larger truth of perception, and the boy evidently

feels, without understanding, the whole symbolized in the part' ('Wordsworth and the Childhood of Language', *Criticism*, 18 (1976), 243–55 (pp. 247–8)).

22 *Poetical Works*, I, 361–2.

23 Don H. Bialostosky, *Making Tales: The Poetics of Wordsworth's Narrative Experiments* (Chicago and London, 1984), p. 116.

24 F.J. Hugo, 'Unity of Mind and the Antagonist Thought of Death in Wordsworth's Poetry', *Theoria*, 51 (October 1979), 15–23 (p. 16).

25 Richard Gravil suggests that the poem parodies evangelical children's rhymes, such as those of Isaac Watts: '*Lyrical Ballads* (1798): Wordsworth as Ironist', *Critical Quarterly*, 24:4 (1982), 39–57 (p. 44).

26 The date 13 July 1798 may be significant. It was 'the anniversary of the day on which Wordsworth first landed in France with Robert Jones, eight years before': J.R. Watson, 'A Note on the Date in the Title of "Tintern Abbey" ', *Wordsworth Circle*, 10 (1979), 379–80.

27 For William Gilpin see Brett and Jones, pp. 296–7; for Hartley's influence see Roper, pp. 274–7; for the challenge posed by 'more' see William Empson, *Seven Types of Ambiguity*, 3rd edition (London, 1953), pp. 151–4.

28 Helen Darbishire first drew atention to the physical vitality of 'along' here (*The Poet Wordsworth* (Oxford, 1950), pp. 164–5): Wordsworth is always aware of the body's machinery, and 'Tintern Abbey' is remarkable for its subtle exploration of the interplay between physical, mental, and emotional, as well as between external and internal.

29 For a summary of the verbal subtleties see Cleanth Brooks and Robert Penn Warren, *Understanding Poetry*, 3rd edition (New York, 1960), pp. 377–80. For 'touch' compare, for example, 'Peter Bell', 286 and (1819 version) 495.

30 The word 'course' is often used of natural order in Wordsworth, and another elegiac use occurs (again associated with the verb 'roll') in the great 'Extempore Effusion Upon the death of James Hogg':

> Nor has the rolling year twice measured,
> From sign to sign, its steadfast course,
> Since every mortal power of Coleridge
> Was frozen at its marvellous source.   (13–16)

31 Because of the later unfortunate associations of 'blooming', it
is worth pointing out that Wordsworth uses it repeatedly to
indicate the poignant freshness of youth. See, for example,
'Peter Bell', 736, and *Excursion*, III, 638.

32 For a good general account of the group see John Garetson
Dings, *The Mind in its Place: Wordsworth, 'Michael' and the
Poetry of 1800* (Salzburg, 1973).

33 See: Stephen Parrish, '*Michael* and the Pastoral Ballad',
Bicentenary Wordsworth Studies in Memory of John Alban Finch,
ed. Jonathan Wordsworth and Beth Darlington (Ithaca, NY,
and London, 1970), pp. 50–75; Jonathan Wordsworth, 'A
Note on the Ballad Version of "Michael"', *Ariel*, 2:2 (April
1971), 66–71; and R.S. Woof, 'Mr Woof's Reply to Mr
Wordsworth', *ibid.*, 72–9.

34 See Beer, p. 183. In a letter of 28 March [1808] Dorothy
Wordsworth says of a Lakeland family: 'They used to sell a
few peats in the summer, which they dug out of their own
heart's heart – their land' (*Letters*, II, 205).

35 Compare 'The Old Cumberland Beggar', 171–2: 'Reverence
the hope whose vital anxiousness / Gives the last human
interest to his heart'.

36 For a strong presentation of the view that Michael sacrifices
Luke (and a penetrating analysis of the powerful 'but' in line
415) see John P. Bushnell, '"Where is the Lamb for a Burnt
Offering?": Michael's Covenant and Sacrifice', *Wordsworth
Circle*, 12 (1981), 246–52. For Luke's name see Peter J.
Manning, '"Michael," Luke, and Wordsworth', *Criticism*, 19
(1977), 195–211.

3   *The Prelude* (1805)

1 *Collected Letters of Samuel Taylor Coleridge*, ed. Earl Leslie
Griggs, 6 vols (Oxford, 1956–71), I, 320–1: [early April 1797],
to Joseph Cottle.

2 *Letters*, VI, 680: [c. 10 April 1839], to Thomas Noon
Talfourd.

3 *Letters*, I, 586: 1 May 1805, to Sir George Beaumont.

4 See also Jeffrey Baker, 'Prelude and Prejudice', *Wordsworth
Circle*, 13 (1982), 79–86.

5 William Empson, *The Structure of Complex Words* (London,

1951), pp. 293–4.

6   *Letters*, I, 586: 1 May 1805, to Sir George Beaumont.

7   See A.C. Bradley's essay 'The Long Poem in the Age of Wordsworth', *Oxford Lectures on Poetry* (London, 1909).

8   The poem employs an extraordinarily complex web of images, including building, seedtime and harvest, home and homecoming, paradise and the Fall. For seedtime and harvest see A.L. French, 'The "Fair Seed-Time" in Wordsworth's *Prelude*', *Critical Review* (Melbourne), 17 (1974), 3–20: this author is also struck by the Hopkins parallel cited below. For home (and much else) see Charles Altieri, 'Wordsworth's Wavering Balance: The Thematic Rhythm of *The Prelude*', *Wordsworth Circle*, 4 (1973), 226–40 (p. 230). It is fair to say that no major aspect of Wordsworth's art has been more neglected: a rigorous study of the subject is urgently needed.

9   G. Wilson Knight, 'The Wordsworthian Profundity', chapter 1 of *The Starlit Dome: Studies in the Poetry of Vision* (London, 1941).

10 Compare, for example, I, 323 and II, 291.

11 D.G. James, *The Romantic Comedy* (London, 1948), p. 150.

12 De Selincourt, p. 198, 11. 27–30; cf. 1850: VI, 427–9.

13 'No worst, there is none', *The Poems of Gerard Manley Hopkins*, ed. W.H. Gardner and N.H. MacKenzie, 4th edition (London, 1967), p. 100.

14 *Poetical Works*, II, 480.

15 *Coleridge's Miscellaneous Criticism*, ed. Thomas Middleton Raysor (London, 1936), pp. 121–6.

16 Perkins, p. 49.

17 For a more problematic approach see Jonathan R. Grandine, *The Problem of Shape in 'The Prelude': The Conflict of Private and Public Speech* (Cambridge, Mass., 1968).

18 Samuel Beckett, 'Tal Coat', *'Proust' and 'Three Dialogues with George Duthuit'* (London, 1965), p. 103.

19 For an excellent discussion of *ethos* and *pathos* see Herbert Lindenberger, *On Wordsworth's 'Prelude'* (Princeton, NJ, 1963), pp. 24ff. See also W.J.B. Owen, 'The Sublime and the Beautiful in *The Prelude*', *Wordsworth Circle*, 4 (1973), 67–86.

20 Perkins shows how such passages derive precision by taking up words from the preceding episodes (p. 214). Also, Frank M. Towne rightly advises readers not to undervalue, in their enthusiasm for the vignettes, the passages describing general

experience: 'Wordsworth's Spiritual Autobiography', *Research
Studies of the State College of Washington*, 25 (1957), 57–62.

21   For the distinction see David Ferry, *The Limits of Mortality:
An Essay on Wordsworth's Major Poems* (Middletown, Conn.,
1959), *passim*.

22   A possible alternative is offered by John F. McCarthy in a fine
article, 'The Conflict in Books I–II of *The Prelude*', *Modern
Language Quarterly*, 30 (1969), 370–85 (p. 383): the 'trouble'
would be 'that sense of alienation which derives from the
awareness of self and other and comes obscurely to the boy
when he begins to seek nature as an object distinct from
himself and a source of voluntary pleasure', and the 'props'
would be his previous harmonious experience of nature:
'Now, without understanding it, he loves the visible world as
a memorial to that lost unity.'

23   Jonathan Wordsworth writes well on the series of falls in the
poem: see 'Fall' in the index to J. Wordsworth.

24   For a useful summary of the role of books in developing
Wordsworth's love of Nature and of humankind see David
Wiener, 'Wordsworth, Books, and the Growth of a Poet's
Mind', *Journal of English and Germanic Philology*, 74 (1975),
209–20.

25   For a stimulating analysis suggesting other structural
possibilities see David V. Boyd, 'Wordsworth as Satirist:
Book VII of *The Prelude*', *Studies in English Literature
1500–1900* (Houston, Texas), 13 (1973), 617–31.

26   Jonathan Wordsworth, *The Music of Humanity* (London,
1969), p. 229.

27   See Jane Worthington, *Wordsworth's Reading of Roman Prose*
(New Haven, Conn., 1946), chapters 1 and 2.

28   1850's division in fact reverts to an earlier plan: *'The Prelude'
1799, 1805, 1850*, ed. Jonathan Wordsworth, M.H. Abrams,
and Stephen Gill (New York and London, 1979), p. 391n.

29   'The impressions of three hours of our walk among the Alps
will never be effaced' (Wordsworth to Dorothy, 6[–16]
September [1790]: *Letters*, I, 33).

30   Ricks, pp. 89–116.

31   Wordsworth's awareness of the importance of line endings is
made clear by a remark of 1804: 'as long as verse shall have
the marked termination that rhyme gives it, and as long as
blank verse shall be printed in lines, it will be Physically

impossible to pronounce the last words or syllables of the
lines with the same indifference, as the others, i.e. not to give
them an intonation of one kind or an other, or to follow them
with a pause, not called out for by the passion of the subject,
but by the passion of metre merely' (*Letters*, I, 434).

32 Perkins, p. 221. Perkins's analysis of the whole crossing
episode is valuable.

33 Susan Luther, 'Wordsworth's *Prelude*, VI. 592–616 (1850)',
Wordsworth Circle, 12 (1981), 253–61.

34 Wallace Jackson observes that such nonsequiturs 'signal the
emotional dislocation of the speaker, indicating that the
emotions evoked by the image pattern have begun to take
over' ('Wordsworth and his Predecessors: Private Sensations
and Public Tones', *Criticism*, 17 (1975), 41–58 (p. 46)).

35 The germ of the expansion was suggested by Coleridge: see
de Selincourt, p. 559.

36 John F. McCarthy, 'The Wordsworthian Imagination in
Poetry: The Simplon Pass and the 1815 Preface', *Discourse*, 12
(1969), 489–514 (pp. 501–2). The *Oxford English Dictionary*
gives 1812 for the last recorded use of 'thwart' meaning
'cross', so that the metaphor was almost, if not quite, dead at
the time of writing.

37 'Dreary' is not a common word in Wordsworth, but on
several of its appearances it is (like 'blank' and 'blind')
associated with the sensory deprivation characteristic of
visionary states. Compare XI, 311 and XII, 317.

4 *Poems, in Two Volumes* (1807)

1 For the significance of 'fancy' and 'imagination' in
Wordsworth see two characteristically astute and thorough
articles by W.J.B. Owen in *The Wordsworth Circle*: 'The
Charm More Superficial', 13 (1982), 8–16, and 'Wordsworth's
Imaginations', 14 (1983), 213–24.

2 *The Poems and Songs of Robert Burns*, ed. Kinsley, 3 vols
(Oxford, 1968), I, 276, 278.

3 *The Edinburgh Review*, 11 (October 1807), 214–31 (p. 218).

4 Wordsworth's use of the word 'mood' varies between
triviality and deep seriousness: contrast, for example, *Prelude*,
II, 383 and XIII, 170.

5   See, for example, 'Hart-Leap Well', 2, and *Prelude*, I, 350.

6   *Biographia*, I, 304 (chapter 13).

7   Geoffrey Durrant, *William Wordsworth* (Cambridge, 1969), chapter 2.

8   'The Picture of little T.C. in a Prospect of Flowers', 23–4: *The Poems and Letters of Andrew Marvell*, ed. H.M. Margoliouth, 3rd edition revised by Pierre Legouis, 2 vols (Oxford, 1971), I, 41.

9   For a possible exception in 'Tintern Abbey' see R.J. Fersch, 'The Wye's "Sweet Inland Murmur"', *Wordsworth Circle*, 16 (1985), 134–5.

10 *Poetical Works*, II, 506.

11 For 'being' see, for example, *Prelude*, II, 420, and Immortality Ode, 158; for 'breath(e)' see *Prelude*, I, 430 and XII, 363.

12 The poem is actually based on a description by Thomas Wilkinson: see Mary Moorman, *William Wordsworth: The Early Years 1770–1803* (Oxford, 1957, corr. 1965), p. 519.

13 *Letters*, I, 650: 29 November [1805], to Lady Beaumont.

14 Geoffrey J. Finch, 'Wordsworth's Solitary Song: The Substance of "true art" in "The Solitary Reaper"', *Ariel*, 6:3 (1975), 91–100 (pp. 99–100).

15 *Letters*, II, 264: 4 August [1808]. Some excuse for Scott may be found in what is probably Dorothy Wordsworth's mistranscription of the poem when sending it to him three years earlier (*Letters*, I, 532).

16 In 1800 it was called 'A Fragment': it is not included in Gill.

17 See, for example, *Prelude*, IV, 472 and V, 463.

18 For an excellent short essay on the sonnets see Carl Woodring, *Wordsworth* (Cambridge, Mass., 1968), chapter 7.

19 Curtis, p. 133n.

20 *Letters*, V, 604–5.

21 J. Hillis Miller, 'The Still Heart: Poetic Form in Wordsworth', *New Literary History*, 2 (1971), 297–310 (pp. 306–7).

22 *Macbeth*, IV. iii. 140ff; *Boswell's Life of Johnson*, ed. George Birkbeck Hill, revised L.F. Powell, 6 vols (Oxford, 1934–50), I, 42.

23 *Letters*, II, 209.

24 The decision to restrict the old man's words was taken in the course of revision before publication: see Curtis, p. 323.

25 For the parallels between poet and leech-gatherer see Robert N. Essick, 'Wordsworth and Leech-Lore', *Wordsworth Circle*,

12 (1981), 100–2.

26 See, for example, *Prelude*, II, 381 and III, 164, and 'On the Departure of Sir Walter Scott', 4–5. Imagination and Fancy are the greater and lesser powers available to the poet: *Prelude*, VIII, 590–2.

27 *Letters*, III, 189.

28 Lionel Trilling, 'The Immortality Ode', in *The Liberal Imagination* (London, 1951).

29 Both adjective and noun 'blank' indicate visionary dereliction: see *Prelude*, I, 422 and (1850) VI, 470 where man endures 'to be lost within himself / In trepidation, from the blank abyss / To look with bodily eyes, and be consoled'.

30 Shelley, 'Prometheus Unbound', II. iv. 116.

31 *The Correspondence of Gerard Manley Hopkins and Richard Watson Dixon*, ed. Claude Colleer Abbott (London, 1935), pp. 147–8: 23 October 1886, quoted by Marcella M. Holloway, CSJ, in 'Hopkins' Defense of Wordsworth's Great Ode', *Hopkins Quarterly*, 5 (1978), 69–74 (p. 70).

5 Conclusion

1 *Letters*, IV, 224: 21 October 1823, to an unknown correspondent.

2 *Letters*, I, 327: 9 April 1801, to Anne Taylor.

3 Mary Moorman, *William Wordsworth, A Biography: The Early Years* (Oxford, 1957, corr. 1965), p. 507.

4 *Biographia*, p. 80 (ch. 4).

5 *Letters*, III, 178: 22 December 1814, to R.P. Gillies.

6 *Letters*, I, 325: 9 April 1801, to John Taylor.

7 *Letters*, I, 367: 14 June [1802], to Sara Hutchinson.

8 *Letters*, II, 383: 4 January [1810], to John Miller.

9 *Letters*, III, 269–70: 12 January 1816.

Suggestions
for Further Reading

A lucid introduction to the intellectual background of Words-worth's poetry is provided by John Purkis, *A Preface to Wordsworth* (2nd edition, London, 1986). John Danby, *The Simple Wordsworth* (London, 1960) is also very stimulating for beginners.

On *Lyrical Ballads* see S.M. Parrish, *The Art of the 'Lyrical Ballads'* (Cambridge, Mass., 1978) and (more difficult) Roger N. Murray, *Wordsworth's Style: Figures and Themes in the 'Lyrical Ballads' of 1800* (Lincoln, Nebr., 1967); on their literary back-ground see Mary Jacobus, *Tradition and Experiment in Wordsworth's 'Lyrical Ballads' (1798)* (Oxford, 1976). For *The Prelude*, Havens's massive study is still useful (see Abbreviated References, p. 143), but a much livelier approach is that of Herbert Lindenberger, *On Wordsworth's 'Prelude'* (Princeton, NJ, 1963). For *Poems, in Two Volumes* see Jared R. Curtis, *Wordsworth's Experiments with Tradition: The Lyric Poems of 1802* (Ithaca, NY, and London, 1971).

All of the critical books listed in the Abbreviated References are recommended for more advanced study, especially Hartman's magisterial apocalyptic work. In addition, David Ferry, *The Limits of Mortality: An Essay on Wordsworth's Major Poems* (Middletown, Conn., 1959) is a seminal treatment of the mystical and sacramental elements. The most approachable and rewarding of post-structuralist studies is David Simpson, *Wordsworth and the Figurings of the Real* (London and Basingstoke, 1982).

Of the earlier criticism, Coleridge's treatment of Wordsworth in *Biographia Literaria* is indispensable, as is Hazlitt's portrait in *The Spirit of the Age*.

The house journal, *The Wordsworth Circle*, is an exceptionally pleasant publication, full of helpful articles, mostly on more restricted subjects but sometimes wide-ranging.

Index

Field, Barron, 6
Finch, Geoffrey J., 111

Gill, Stephen, 140
Gilpin, William, 38
Godwin, William, 21, 84

Hamilton, William, of Bangour,
  113
Hartley, David, 38
Hartman, Geoffrey, 110, 133
Hazlitt, William, 1, 19–20
Hopkins, Gerard Manley, 58,
  137–8
Hugo, F.J., 9, 36
Hutchinson, Sara, 123

James, King VI and I, 122
James, D.G., 57
Jeffrey, Francis, 1, 5, 19, 23, 97–8
Johnson, Samuel, 54
Jones, Robert, 74
Jonson, Ben, 94
Joyce, James, 58
Juvenal (Decimus Junius
  Juvenalis), 55

Keats, John, 140; *The Fall of
  Hyperion*, 57, 123; 'Ode on a
  Grecian Urn', 135; 'On First
  Looking into Chapman's
  Homer', 125
Knight, G. Wilson, 56

Lamb, Charles, 3

McCarthy, John F., 92
McCracken, David, 15
The Maid of Buttermere, 76, 78
Marvell, Andrew: 'The Picture of
  little T.C. in a Prospect of
  Flowers', 108
Miller, J. Hillis, 121
Milton, John, 9, 88, 119; 'On His
  Blindness', 63; *Paradise Lost*, 7,
  48, 54–5, 62, 82
Montagu, Basil (father), 27
Montagu, Basil (son), 31
Murray, Roger N., 8

Ossian, 114–15

Palmer, Samuel, 30
Perkins, David, 88
Petrarch, Francesco, 119, 124
Piero della Francesca, 45
Pope, Alexander: *Moral Essays*, 76

Ray, Martha, 27, 31
Richardson, Samuel, 25
Ricks, Christopher, 88
Robespierre, Maximilien, 83

Scott, Sir Walter, 10; *Marmion*,
  10, 113
Shakespeare, William, 9, 88, 119;
  Antony and Cleopatra, 107–8;
  Hamlet, 109; *King Lear*, 107–8;
  Macbeth, 122
Shelley, Percy Bysshe, 120;
  Prometheus Unbound, 137
Southey, Robert, 4, 18
Sterne, Laurence: *Tristram
  Shandy*, 60
Stravinsky, Igor, 45

Taylor, William, 83
Trilling, Lionel, 134
Turner, Joseph Mallord William,
  120
Tyson, Ann, 70

Vallon, Annette, 27, 55, 82, 125

Wilson, John ('Christopher
  North'), 1–2, 19, 28
Wither, George, 94; *The
  Shepherd's Hunting. Eclogue 4*,
  94–5
Woolf, Virginia: *To the
  Lighthouse*, 93
Wordsworth, Dorothy, 3, 22, 27,
  31, 33, 36–7, 48, 69, 74, 82, 84,
  86, 101, 106–8, 110, 125
Wordsworth, John, 4, 130, 140
Wordsworth, Jonathan, 79
Wordsworth, Mary, 74, 106,
  108–10